RSYA

21.95

COMPREHENSIVE RESEARCH
AND STUDY GUIDE

H.D.

BLOOM'S

MAJOR

POETS

EDITED AND WITH AN INTRODUCTION
BY HAROLD BLOOM

CURRENTLY AVAILABLE

BLOOM'S MAJOR DRAMATISTS	BLOOM'S MAJOR NOVELISTS	BLOOM'S MAJOR POETS	BLOOM'S MAJOR SHORT STORY WRITERS
Aeschylus	Jane Austen	Maya Angelou	Jorge Louis Borges
Aristophanes	The Brontës	Elizabeth Bishop	Italo Calvino
Bertold Brecht	Willa Cather	William Blake	Raymond Carver
Anton Chekhov	Stephen Crane	Gwendolyn Brooks	Anton Chekhov
Henrik Ibsen	Charles Dickens	Robert Browning	Joseph Conrad
Ben Johnson	William Faulkner	Geoffrey Chaucer	Stephen Crane
Christopher Marlowe	F. Scott Fitzgerald	Sameul Taylor Coleridge	William Faulkner
Arthur Miller	Nathaniel Hawthorne	Dante	F. Scott Fitzgerald
Eugene O'Neill	Ernest Hemingway	Emily Dickinson	Nathaniel Hawthorne
Shakespeare's Comedies	Henry James	John Donne	Ernest Hemingway
Shakespeare's Histories	James Joyce	H.D.	O. Henry
Shakespeare's Romances	D. H. Lawrence	T. S. Eliot	Shirley Jackson
Shakespeare's Tragedies	Toni Morrison	Robert Frost	Henry James
George Bernard Shaw	John Steinbeck	Seamus Heaney	James Joyce
Neil Simon	Stendhal	Homer	Franz Kafka
Oscar Wilde	Leo Tolstoy	Langston Hughes	D.H. Lawrence
Tennessee Williams	Mark Twain	John Keats	Jack London
August Wilson	Alice Walker	John Milton	Thomas Mann
	Edith Wharton	Sylvia Plath	Herman Melville
	Virginia Woolf	Edgar Allan Poe	Flannery O'Connor
		Poets of World War I	Edgar Allan Poe
		Shakespeare's Poems & Sonnets	Katherine Anne Porter
		Percy Shelley	J. D. Salinger
		Alfred, Lord Tennyson	John Steinbeck
		Walt Whitman	Mark Twain
		William Carlos Williams	John Updike
		William Wordsworth	Eudora Welty
		William Butler Yeats	

COMPREHENSIVE RESEARCH
AND STUDY GUIDE

H.D.

BLOOM'S *MAJOR* POETS

EDITED AND WITH AN INTRODUCTION
BY HAROLD BLOOM

First Printing
1 3 5 7 9 8 6 4 2

Library of Congress Cataloging-in-Publication Data
H.D. / Harold Bloom, ed..
        p. cm. —(Bloom's major poets)
Includes bibliographical references and index.
    1. H. D. (Hilda Doolittle), 1886–1961—Criticism and
interpretation.
I. Title: HD. II Bloom, Harold. III. Series.
    PS3507.0726 Z695 2002
    811'.52—dc21   2002004388

ISBN 0-7910-6817-X
Chelsea House Publishers
1974 Sproul Road, Suite 400
Broomall, PA 19008-0914

The Chelsea House World Wide Web address is http://www.chelseahouse.com

Contributing Editor: Camille-Yevette Welsch

Layout by EJB Publishing Services

CONTENTS

USER'S GUIDE

This volume is designed to present biographical, critical, and bibliographical information on the author and the author's best-known or most important short stories. Following Harold Bloom's editor's note and introduction is a concise biography of the author that discusses major life events and important literary accomplishments. A plot summary of each story follows, tracing significant themes, patterns, and motifs in the work. An annotated list of characters supplies brief information on the main characters in each story. As with any study guide, it is recommended that the reader read the story beforehand, and have a copy of the story being discussed available for quick reference.

A selection of critical extracts, derived from previously published material, follows each character list. In most cases, these extracts represent the best analysis available from a number of leading critics. Because these extracts are derived from previously published material, they will include the original notations and references when available. Each extract is cited, and readers are encouraged to check the original publication as they continue their research. A bibliography of the author's writings, a list of additional books and articles on the author and their work, and an index of themes and ideas conclude the volume.

ABOUT THE EDITOR

Harold Bloom is Sterling Professor of the Humanities at Yale University and Henry W. and Albert A. Berg Professor of English at the New York University Graduate School. He is the author of over 20 books, and the editor of more than 30 anthologies of literary criticism.

Professor Bloom's works include *Shelly's Mythmaking* (1959), *The Visionary Company* (1961), *Blake's Apocalypse* (1963), *Yeats* (1970), *A Map of Misreading* (1975), *Kabbalah and Criticism* (1975), *Agon: Toward a Theory of Revisionism* (1982), *The American Religion* (1992), *The Western Canon* (1994), and *Omens of Millennium: The Gnosis of Angels, Dreams, and Resurrection* (1996). *The Anxiety of Influence* (1973) sets forth Professor Bloom's provocative theory of the literary relationships between the great writers and their predecessors. His most recent books include *Shakespeare: The Invention of the Human*, a 1998 National Book Award finalist, *How to Read and Why* (2000), and *Stories and Poems for Extremely Intelligent Children of All Ages* (2001).

Professor Bloom earned his Ph.D. from Yale University in 1955 and has served on the Yale faculty since then. He is a 1985 MacArthur Foundation Award recipient and served as the Charles Eliot Norton Professor of Poetry at Harvard University in 1987–88. In 1999 he was awarded the prestigious American Academy of Arts and Letters Gold Medal for Criticism. Professor Bloom is the editor of several other Chelsea House series in literary criticism, including BLOOM'S MAJOR SHORT STORY WRITERS, BLOOM'S MAJOR NOVELISTS, BLOOM'S MAJOR DRAMATISTS, MODERN CRITICAL INTERPRETATIONS, MODERN CRITICAL VIEWS, and BLOOM'S BIOCRITIQUES.

EDITOR'S NOTE

My Introduction attempts to engage H.D. at her crisis-center, and therefore deals with two poems not otherwise discussed in this volume, "The Master," her vision of Sigmund Freud, who had analyzed her, and "The Poet," her account of D.H. Lawrence, with whom her friendship failed.

I will cite only a few of the distinguished "Critical Views" here, so as to highlight some of the difficulties of H.D. criticism. Cassandra Laity usefully shows the effect of the Decadents upon H.D.'s erotic vision in "Orchard," while Susan Gubar and Eileen Gregory relate Sappho to "Fragment 113."

Diana Collecott illuminates "Helen" by showing the evolution of the figure in H.D.'s poetry, after which Susan Stanford Freidman analyzes "The Walls Do Not Fall."

"Tribute to the Angels" is seen by Albert Gelpi as giving us H.D.'s fundamental idealization of woman, while Joseph Riddell demonstrates the way in which H.D. constructs her most characteristic images.

Harold Bloom

There is something quaintly archaic about H.D.'s *Tribute to Freud*, where the Professor's interventions are so accurate, his spiritual efficacy so instantaneous, as to suggest the advent of a new age of faith, the Freud era. A prose memorial provokes our resistances when it seems too pious or too amiably earnest. The pre-Raphaelite aura, hieratic and isolated, with its characteristic effect of a hard-edged phantasmagoria, rescues "The Master" from the cloying literalism of the *Tribute*. "The old man" of the poem is God's prophet, since "the dream is God," and Freud therefore is heard as one who speaks with authority: "his command/ was final" and "his tyranny was absolute,/ for I had to love him then." The command, at least as H.D. interpreted it, was to accept her own bisexuality as being one with her poethood:

> I do not know what to say to God,
> for the hills
> answer his nod,
> and the sea
> when he tells his daughter,
> white Mother
> of green
> leaves
> and green rills
> and silver,
> to still
> tempest
> or send peace
> and surcease of peril
> when a mountain has spit fire:
>
> I did not know how to differentiate
> between volcanic desire,
> anemones like embers
> and purple fire
> of violets
> like red heat,
> and the cold

silver
of her feet:

I had two loves separate;
God who loves all mountains,
alone knew why
and understood
and told the old man
to explain

the impossible,

which he did.
                        ("The Master")

    The phallic or volcanic is evidently preferred by this male God, at least rhetorically, but of the "two loves separate" the "cold/ silver/ of her feet" triumphs with the re-entry of the dancer in section 5. The force that comes with celebration of the dancer depends upon H.D.'s vision of herself as wrestling Jacob, arguing till daybreak, and of Freud as God or His angel, giving further rhetorical primacy to "the man-strength" rather than to the dancer's leapings:

I was angry with the old man
with his talk of the man-strength,
I was angry with his mystery, his mysteries,
I argued till day-break

O, it was late,
and God will forgive me, my anger,
but I could not accept it.

I could not accept from wisdom
what love taught,
woman is perfect.
                        ("The Dancer")

    That would appear to have meant that a woman's bisexuality or her perfection (in the sense of completeness) was of a different and more acceptable order than a man's bisexuality. The ecstasy of section 5 gently mocks the Freudian "man-strength" even as it salutes the dancer for needing no male, since at least as dancer (or poet) woman is indeed pragmatically perfect. Section 5 has a kind of uncanny force, akin to Yeatsian celebrations of the dancer as image. But the authentic strength of the poem centers elsewhere, in its elegiac identifications of the dead father, Freud, with the earth, and with all the dead fathers. Freud is Saturn, ancient wisdom, and the rock that cannot be broken—a new earth. His temples will be everywhere, yet H.D. cries out: "only I, I will escape," an escape sanctioned by Freud as the freedom of the woman poet. Though D.H. Lawrence is not even alluded to in "The Master," he enters the poem by negation, since it is transformed into a fierce hymn against Lawrence's vision of sexual release:

> no man will be present in those mysteries,
> yet all men will kneel,
> no man will be potent,
> important,
> yet all men will feel
> what it is to be a woman,
> will yearn,
> burn,
> turn from easy pleasure
> to hardship
> of the spirit,
>
> men will see how long they have been blind,
> poor men
> poor man-kind
> how long
> how long
> this thought of the man-pulse has tricked them.
> has weakened them,
> shall see woman,
> perfect.
>
> ("The Master")

The blindness is precisely Lawrence's in H.D.'s judgment, and it is hinted at, in muted form, in "The Poet," not so much an elegy for Lawrence as for her failed friendship with him. What seems clear is that her sexual self-acceptance, whether Freudian or not, gave her the creative serenity that made possible the wonderfully controlled, hushed resignation of her wisely limited farewell to Lawrence:

> No,
> I don't pretend, in a way, to understand,
> nor know you,
> nor even see you;

I say,
"I don't grasp his philosophy,
and I don't understand,"

but I put out a hand, touch a cold door,
(we have both come from so far);
I touch something imperishable;
I think,
why should he stay there?
why should he guard a shrine so alone,
so apart,
on a path that leads nowhere?

he is keeping a candle burning in a shrine
where nobody comes,
there must be some mystery
in the air
about him,

he couldn't live alone in the desert,
without vision to comfort him,
there must be voices somewhere.
("The Poet")

The wistfulness of that tribute, if it is a tribute, veils the harshness of the critique. A woman can be perfect, but a man cannot, though Lawrence would not learn this. One can imagine his response to H.D.; it would have been violent, but that perhaps would have confirmed her stance, whether sanctioned or unsanctioned by her father and master, Freud.

H.D.

Hilda Doolittle, or more famously, H.D. found herself in the middle three major movements of twentieth century literary history: Imagism, Modernism and Freudianism. Until recently, H.D. was most often read as an imagist, an idea complicit with her easily anthologized short poems of the early portion of her career. In reality, H.D. was a somewhat reluctant imagist, who soon grew out of the movement as her writing matured into the longer, book length poems which, like the work of her childhood companions and modernist peers, Ezra Pound and W.C. Williams, explored loss of faith in old systems of faith and knowledge and new modes of articulation in modernity.

H.D. was born in Bethlehem, Pennsylvania, on September 10, 1886, to a scientist father and an artistic mother. She inherited a dual nature, which in many ways accounted for her interest in religion, poetry and psychoanalysis. From her mother's family, she grew up steeped in the Moravian religion, a faith rich in image and mysticism that created in H.D. a fascination with religion and its symbolism. At the age of ten, her parents moved to Upper Darby, Pennsylvania, so that her father might take a job teaching at the University of Pennsylvania. In 1901, H.D. met Pound and they became friends and sweethearts, later becoming engaged, then disengaged at least twice. Around that same time, she met and became friends with William Carlos Williams, who was also a student at the University of Pennsylvania. Both men, particularly Pound, would influence her writing. In 1905, H.D. began schooling at Bryn Mawr then left the next year due to illness. She remained home and studied over the next few years while Pound went to school, and worked. The two met again in New York and he urged her to follow him to London. She followed him and never again lived in the United States.

Once in London, she discovered that Pound had engaged himself to another woman, and though H.D. called off their engagement, the two still traveled and studied together, staying active in London's literary scene and remaining lifelong friends. In 1912, H.D. showed Pound two of her poems, which Pound quite famously declared to be

Imagist poems. After some brief editing, and a name change from Hilda Doolittle to H.D., the poet found herself launched in the literary world when the poems appeared in *Poetry* the next year. During those early years in London, Pound introduced H.D. to several literary figures, among them poet, Richard Aldington, who she married in 1913. Aldington introduced her to D.H. Lawrence with whom she later had an intense affair, both literary and otherwise.

In 1915, H.D. gave birth to a stillborn daughter; the death affected her deeply. That same year, Aldington enlisted, distancing himself further from his wife and encouraging her to have affairs with other men. In 1918, she lost her brother in World War I, and found herself destitute, pregnant, very ill and completely alone, having been deserted by both her husband and the father of her child, Cecil Gray. Her new friend and admirer of her work, who would become her companion and many argue, lover, Winnifred Ellerman (Bryher) stepped into the void created by the men in H.D.'s life. She supported the poet both financially and emotionally for the rest of their lives. In 1919, when H.D. gave birth to a daughter, Perdita Schaffner, Bryher helped her through it. That same year, the poet lost her father, another loss in a series of devastating losses that she associated with the War. When she later became an analysand of Freud, she worked through her fear of war, a fear closely related with these deaths.

Professionally, H.D. thrived. Her work had appeared in Imagist Anthologies throughout the teens and her first book, *Sea Garden,* was published in 1916 to good critical reception. That same year she served as literary editor of *The Egoist*, replacing her husband during his tour of duty. Though most critics viewed her in terms of the Imagist tenets, her trademark revisionist myth-making tendencies were already showing. Between 1919 and 1923, H.D. and Bryher traveled extensively, during which time H.D. had two visions that would figure prominently in her later work as symbols incorporated into her personal mythology. In 1921, she published *Hymen*, which, like its predecessor met with critical acclaim. However, in this volume, H.D. was clearly moving away from Imagism through her use of personae, although the exacting nature of her rhythms still met with the Imagist imperative. She published *Heliodora & Other Poems* in 1924, which, combined with the two earlier volumes, became *Collected Poems* in 1925.

For the next several years, H.D. split her interest between novels and the cinema, a media she admired for its use of image. Critically, H.D.'s fiction fizzled. Critics felt it esoteric and linguistically gimmicky, but the palimpsest and hieroglyph metaphors, her notions of the sacred and her interest in the syncretist tradition introduced in her novels, became an integral part of her later poetry. Her novels also prove useful in examining her personal life as they directly mirrored it.

In 1931, *Red Roses For Bronze* was released and, like the novels, found scant critical interest. She wrote little between 1932 to 1942. She chose instead to focus on researching the hermetic tradition and participating in psychoanalysis. In 1933, she became Freud's analysand, an experience she wrote about in *Tribute to Freud*. Famously, the two argued the existence of God and the true nature of H.D. as an artist. He encouraged her to write, believing her a 'true' artist. 1938 proved bittersweet; H.D. officially divorced Aldington and won the Levinson prize for poetry. In the next year, she moved back to London where she remained for the Second World War. During this time, she conceived and wrote what many consider to be one of her strongest pieces, which, although it was originally published in three parts, has come to be thought of as one multi-faceted poem, *Trilogy*. In this poem, H.D. finally realized her potential as poet-prophet and feminist revisionist.

The war proved to be a period of intense production for the poet, she wrote a novel and drafted her *Tribute to Freud*. Unfortunately, the stress of war brought on a mental breakdown and H.D. left London to rest in Switzerland. The rest proved fruitful and H.D. published *By Avon River* in 1949. The war also proved the breaking point for the relationship between H.D. and Bryher. The two women separated in 1946 though they remained in constant contact for the rest of their lives.

In the fifties, H.D. became good friends within Norman Holmes Pearson, who counseled her on her writing and arranged for her papers to be left to Yale's Beineke Library. He encouraged her to revise her notes on Pound into a book, *End to Torment* which he edited after her death. With his assistance, she published two more major works before her death, both intensely autobiographical, the loosely veiled novel, *Bid Me To Live*, and the revisionist myth poem,

Helen in Egypt. Helen has been embraced by contemporary critics for its feminist heros and re-visionary mythmaking. A year before her death, H.D. received the Award of Merit Medal for Poetry. It marked her last trip to the States.

Eleven years after her death, *Hermetic Definitions* was published, the first of seven posthumously published works. Due to the length and the depth of allusion in H.D.'s poetry and her literary affiliations, she is often thought to be a poet's poet, appreciated only by those in the Academy; however, with the breadth of feminist criticism, H.D. is slowly being rediscovered.

"Orchard"

Originally titled "Priapus" with the sub-title, "Keeper of the Orchards," the poem appeared in Poetry in January 1913 and appeared, re-titled "Orchard" in *Sea-Garden* in 1925. The story surrounding the poem remains steeped in literary legend. In April 1912, HD met with long-time friend and former fiancée, Ezra Pound at the tea room in London's British museum. When Pound read her two poems, "Priapus" and "Hermes of the Ways," H.D. writes in *End to Torment* he turned to her and said, "'But Dryad, (in the Museum tea room) this is poetry.' He slashed with a pencil. 'Cut this out, shorten this line. 'Hermes of the Ways' is a good title. I'll send it to Harriet Monroe of *Poetry*. Have you a copy? Yes? Then we can send this, or I'll type it when we get back. Will this do?' And he scrawled H.D. Imagiste at the bottom of the page."[1] With this somewhat dictatorial move by Pound, H.D. found herself representing the ideas of Imagism.

Essentially, Imagism espouses a few central tenets: the use of free verse, clear, concentrated images devoid of sentimental association, and the integration of common speech cadences and patterns. Certainly, "Orchard" fulfills this criteria; however, H.D.'s use of myth complicates it somewhat as it moves beyond what Pound referred to as the "direct treatment of the thing," it moves into the history of the image as well. This insistence on understanding origin and the way in which it relates to the treatment of the "thing" proves a pervasive quality in H.D.'s poetry.

The poem, like so many others, demands a knowledge of Greek myth. Priapus, popularly believed to be the son of Dionysus and Aphrodite, was the god of fertility in nature, protector of the orchard and the garden, guardian of male fertility. In most representations, artists and writers alike depict him as possessing a huge phallus, continuously erect, representative of his potency. The rest of Priapus stands in stark contrast to this constant masculine assertion. Apparently while in utero, Hera cursed Aphrodite's baby making him ugly, his body grossly disproportionate. The sheer unattractive-

---

[1]H.D., *End to Torment*, (New York Directions, 1979): p. 18.

ness of the child deeply offended Aphrodite's sensibility and she left the baby in the forest where a herdsman eventually found and took him in, realizing that everywhere Priapus went, things were sure to grow. His power swayed both animals and plants to procreate like mad. In his role as protector, Priapus felt more than free to use the size of his genitals to strike fear of sodomy in those that might trespass into the garden or orchard. Priapus also served as a protector of men and tutor to Ares the war god, teaching him both to dance and to fight. In addition to the prominence of his member, Priapus can also frequently be seen holding a drinking cup and the fruits of the fertility he inspired, making him both a comic figure and a figure profoundly revered.

The title of the poem, "Orchard," offers an immediate notion of setting. Couple that with the original title, "Priapus," and the reader immediately understands to whom the direct address is given. H.D. begins recounting the first fall of the fruit, immediately evoking loose associations with the Fall, associations which will resonate throughout the poem. This interest in syncretism pervades the body of H.D.'s poetry. Immediately after the fall of the over-ripe fruit, bees swarm in to partake of its juicy splendor:

> he honey-seeking, golden-banded,
> the yellow swarm
> was not more fleet than I,
> (spare us from your loveliness).

Though she makes a valiant effort to save the fruit, she is unsuccessful, the bees plunder the fruit, mimicking the act of procreation under the watchful eye of Priapus to whom the distraught poet sends her cry. Neither she, nor the fruit, are spared from the fertility rites, from the overabundance of blossoms and fruits, from the subsequent attack upon them. For the narrator, loveliness, indeed maturation, brings with it a dual fear, one of ravishment and the other of growing beyond the fertile years, particularly for women who are often defined by fertility. In the face of such beauty, such waste, and such brutality as surrounds the fallen fruit, the poet can take no other recourse but to fall to the ground, "prostrate/ crying:/." Again, she addresses Priapus, both to accuse and to beg:

> you have flayed us
> with your blossoms,
> spare us the beauty
> of fruit trees.

The poet protests the abundance, the endless procreative facilities, the sheer range of beauty gone to waste.

Still, in the midst of all her protests and her rage,

> The honey-seeking
> paused not,
> the air thundered their song,
> and I alone was prostrate.

The ravishment continues, unheeded by the ceaseless procreative quest of the bees, an easy comparison to the quest of the men in H.D.'s life, particularly her former fiancee, Pound, who knew that the prostrate poet remained a virgin at twenty-five despite his machinations. A second reading might suggest that H.D. herself felt overwhelmed by the idea of this insistent, demanding sexual aggression and found herself prostrate in the face of it, begging only that the beauty, possibly her own physical beauty, be taken away so that she might again have peace. She goes so far as to make an entreaty and an offering to the god:

> O rough-hewn
> god of the orchard,
> I bring you an offering—
> do you, alone unbeautiful, son of the god,
> spare us from loveliness:

The narrator, ostensibly the poet, appeals to the emotions of the god, referring to his ugliness in the midst of so much beauty, to gain sympathy for her cause. There is the suggestion that Priapus's displaced powers of fertility make up for his own lack of beauty, an idea in which he furiously participated. It is to this insecurity that the poet seems to be appealing. Then she begins to list her offering. Here, the specificity of language and sensory detail fully supports the Imagist ideals:

> those fallen hazel-nuts,
> stripped late of their green sheaths,
> grapes, red-purple,

their berries
dripping with wine,
pomegranates already broken,
and shrunken figs
and quinces untouched,

She lists a cornacopia of consequence. The over-ripe fruit is broken, bleeding and burst. The quinces and figs have collapsed into themselves, the nuts lay naked in the garden. Beauty and death co-exist here. The fertility that once held so much promise has wasted away, overdone in its own eagerness, a death fomented by Priapus and his burden of procreativity. All are left to die without being savored, a fate from which the poet hopes to except herself by removing the compulsory impulse.

Here, the correlation with the Christian myth of the Fall takes on new resonance. With the advent of sexuality and fertility comes death, as it has come to the offerings in the poem. The parallel to the Fall of man and the introduction of the fig leaf are clear. Still, H.D. refuses to offer a sole exit to the poem. The poem ends with the line, "I bring you as offering." Syntactically, it should be the hazel-nuts and various sundries which she offers, leaving it clear that the poet has not tried to dethrone the god, and, instead, is prostrating herself before him in the hopes that his power can help her, perhaps to be savored herself, perhaps to offer a rebirth to the produce.

Still, after eight lines, the origin of the offering becomes unclear and the line reads ambiguously. Perhaps the "you" becomes a direct object rather than the object of the preposition. The items are no longer brought to the god, instead, he, himself, becomes the offering, perhaps the most poignant example of the over-ripe and undersated. Also, the anaphoric effect of "I bring you an offering—" and the final "I bring you as offering." suggests that the phrases refer to each other. With that being the case, the repetition reinforces the project of the poem, to protest the insistence on procreation to the detriment of those unwillingly engaged or unwilling to engage. Priapus becomes not only the purveyor of sexuality but the purveyed by the end, placing him in the same position as the reluctant poet.

"Orchard"

JANICE S. ROBINSON ON H.D., POUND AND THE
TROUBADOUR TRADITION

[Janice S. Robinson is the author of *H.D.: The Life and Work of an American Poet*. In this chapter, she discusses H.D.'s identification of Pound with Priapus as a mockery of his ascription to the troubadour ideals for men and bards.]

While H.D.'s "Priapus" attains a beauty that W. R. Paton's English translations in the Loeb Classical Library edition of the *Anthology* do not, its beauty does not preclude the possibility of humor and irony. H.D.'s "Priapus" is, in fact, an ironic comment upon Pound's phallic/poetic pursuits. There is a section of the *Anthology* titled "Dedicatory Epigrams," in which the Greeks dedicate the tools of their youthful trade to the gods. In the manner of these epigrams, H.D. assumes the pose of a courtesan grown old and in her "Priapus" dedicates the gifts of her trade, "her womanly charms." She offers "pomegranates already broken,/And shrunken fig,/And quinces untouched," which we immediately recognize as traditional symbols of feminine sexuality.

Thus, when H.D. tells us in the headnote to the poem that "Priapus" is "from the anthology," she is indicating that it at one level derives from epigrams such as those written by Crinagoras and Leonidas and at another brings an offering to the phallic god similar to those of the epigrams—nuts, pomegranates, grapes, and so on.

The stunning clarity of the images presented in H.D.'s early poems was the quality that drew the immediate attention of poets and critics alike. The humorous and ironic quality of "Priapus" was largely unnoticed (except perhaps by Pound). The fundamental irony of H.D.'s poem lies in its relation to the underlying biographical reality as well as in the allusions to the epigrams of the *Anthology*, for the fact of the situation was that H.D. was by temperament and upbringing the very opposite of the courtesan that she felt that Pound was encouraging her to become; she was, as Pound knew, still a virgin at the age of twenty-five.

Like most irony, H.D.'s is of course deadly serious. In the act of writing these poems she was disentangling herself from Pound for good, regardless of how much it hurt either of them. She had had enough, and in a psychic sense chose survival rather than annihilation. Pound could not seem to understand that his romantic plan was a gross insult to H.D. In its January 1913 appearance in *Poetry*, "Priapus" was given the subtitle "Keeper of Orchards" in recognition of the fact that Priapus (Pound) was a keeper of more than one woman—or, shall we say, a keeper of a goodly number of "trees." When the poem appeared in H.D.'s *Collected Poems* in 1925, it was titled simply "Orchard."

"Priapus" is in fact something of a mockery of the troubadour tradition. This makes it all the more amusing that Pound should help publish it as H.D.'s entrance into the world of poetry. The poem calls into question both the troubadour tradition of poetry.

—Janice S. Robinson, "'Priapus' and 'Hermes.'" *H.D.: The Life and Work of an American Poet* (Boston: Houghton Mifflin, 1982): pp. 30–1.

CYRENA N. PONDROM ON H.D.'S INFLUENCE ON IMAGISM AND MODERNISM

[Cyrena N. Pondrom is a Professor of English and Women's Studies at the University of Wisconsin-Madison. She is the author of *The Road from Paris: French Influence on English Poetry, 1900–1920*. Using 'Orchard' as an example in terms of technique and history, Pondrom places H.D. as both a Modernist and an Imagist, focusing on the idea that H.D. was more of a central figure to the movements then critics suggest.]

The imagist poems of H.D. stand in sharp contrast to these early poems of Pound and Aldington in clarity, sharpness, precision, objectivity, and use of a presentational rather than a discursive style. All three poems that she published in January, 1913, use figures drawn from Greek mythology (as does Aldington's "Choricos"), but in a fashion as concrete as the original epics or stories. The poem entitled "Priapus" and subtitled "Keeper of Orchards," for example, begins:

> I saw the first pear
> As it fell.
> The honey-seeking, golden-banded,
> The yellow swarm
> Was not more fleet than I,
> (Spare us from loveliness!)
> And I fell prostrate,
> Crying,
> Thou hast flayed us with thy blossoms;
> Spare us the beauty
> Of fruit-trees!

The prayer is to Priapus, the son of Dionysus and Aphrodite, and thus offspring of revelry and love. He is the god of fruitfulness, the protector of the bees, the vine, the garden. He was represented in sculpture as the phallus or as a small garden god with twisted body and huge penis. The poem presents a moment in the orchard at harvest time, a moment fraught with intense and conflicting emotions.

It is the inevitable instant at which the ripeness of the maturing fruit passes from the conclusion of growth to the beginning of decay. It is the moment at which the fruit is at its sweetest. This swelling, fecund fruit is primal—it is the first pear—and its fall is primal too. Its uterine shape invokes the female gift for reproduction as the phallic god of the garden invokes the male. The speaker in the poem speeds by sight to the place of fall with the swiftness of the bees ("The honey-seeking, golden banded,/The yellow-swarm"), whom Priapus protects, who come to make honey from fruit. The very act of seeing is an expression of passionate desire to apprehend that moment—its beauty, its meaning, its fruit. Made analogous to the bees by the identity of action, the speaker too seems about to recreate that moment into something sweet, something with the power to nourish and please. At that very moment of apprehension there is another apprehension, the recognition of the intense experience of plenitude, ripeness (perhaps, in a subtext, even of birth itself) as threat: ("Spare us from loveliness!").

Like the pear, the speaker falls—"prostrate,/Crying." The possible meanings of the fall and tears are many, and all are a part of the exegesis of that moment. The loveliness may be too great, the experience too intense, so that at the moment of its apprehension the ecstasy cannot be distinguished from pain. The moment of fruition may contain the recognition of destruction, and the experience of the greatest loveliness may make the inevitability of its loss through decay unbearable. The fall may be complete submission to the beauty perceived, and the tears the tears of joyous apprehension. Again, the fall may be the primal human fall, brought about by eating of the fruit of the tree of the knowledge of good and evil; the act of seeing the beauty and death in the moment of the pear's fall may be the modern counterpart to that ancient myth of overreaching. The fall may be a sexual fall, and the tears the reflection both of joy at that moment and anguish at its power to flay and to consume. The structure of the poem invites all these suggestions, and the poem derives its significance from the complicated sum of all of these endlessly interacting meanings.

The second stanza identifies this paradoxical moment of conflicting emotions as the peculiar triumph or affliction of the human speaker:

> The honey-seeking
> Paused not,
> The air thundered their song,
> And I alone was prostrate.

The speaker next renews the petition to the "God of the orchard" to "Spare us from loveliness" and pledges an offering. That offering is enumerated in the fourth and final stanza:

> The fallen hazel-nuts,
> Stripped late of their green sheaths,
> The grapes, red-purple,
> Their berries
> Dripping with wine,
> Pomegranates already broken,
> And shrunken fig,
> And quinces untouched,
> I bring thee as offering.

These offerings are of fruits past their prime; the grapes have begun to ferment, the pomegranates are broken, and the womb-like fig has lost its ripe fullness. These fruits, like the untouched quinces, were not consumed in their ripeness. They are an appropriate gift from one praying to be spared the moment of consuming intensity. The implication that the cost of escape from that moment is to die without being savoured again suggests a sexual subtext; the experiences that loveliness brings are anguishing, but the cost of escaping them is barrenness or infertility. In early fall, 1912, when H.D. showed this poem to Pound, her own life was fraught with just such anguishing conflicts. Engaged to Pound before he left for Europe in 1908, H.D. in 1910 had become seriously involved with Frances Gregg. It was with Frances and her mother that H.D. had made the journey to Europe in 1911, from which H.D. was never permanently to return to the United States. Pound himself apparently also became involved with Gregg—one friend recalled him as "engaged" to her. Throughout 1912, H.D. was constantly in the company of Pound and Aldington, whom she would not marry until 1913. It seems clear that in 1911 and 1912 H.D. was torn, both between heterosexual and homosexual attractions and between personal poetic creativity and the role of handmaiden and muse which she felt Pound thrust upon her. Each sexual alternative must have seemed to offer anguish which could be escaped only at the cost of physical or poetic barrenness. The intensity of experience which this poem captures, then, has its correlative in H.D.'s own life, but the control she gains through the embodiment of the experience in juxtaposed images epitomizes the "objectivity" which came to be identified as a hallmark of modernism.

—Cyrena N. Pondrom, "H.D. and the Origins of Imagism." *Sagetrieb* 4:1 (Spring 1985): pp. 83–85.

CASSANDRA LAITY ON THE INFLUENCE OF THE DECADENTS

[Cassandra Laity is an Assistant Professor of English at Drew University. She is the author of *H.D. and the Victorian Fin De Siècle*. Here, she explores the effect of the Decadents on H.D.'s creation of romantic landscapes and her treatment of sexual politics.]

The early Imagist landscapes of H.D.'s *Sea Garden* demonstrate her debt to the Romantic overflowered paradise and regenerate landscape as projections of obstructed or liberated states of mind. *Sea Garden* establishes a dialectic between the dense "sheltered garden" that "chokes out life" and the dynamic "wind-tortured" seascapes of triumphant, glinting flowers and distant rock terraces. In poems such as "Garden" and "Sheltered Garden," H.D. images the psychic paralysis traditionally associated with the Romantic Venusberg. Usually oversweet, overflowered and located in an enclosed space—a garden, bower, or glade—the Romantic fallen paradise of love from Keats through the Pre-Raphaelites, Decedents and early Yeats, conceals a deadly trap behind its apparently safe, sensuous refuge. Its dense, enclosed atmosphere proves stifling rather than protective; frequently overripe, the lush vegetation suggests the cloying sweetness of decay. Despite its sensuous promise, the love bower is actually sterile and blighting in its all-consuming torpor which anesthetizes its victim, overpowering all generative impulses, including sexual desire. As a metaphoric projection for mental processes, the garden signifies stasis, escapism, and psychic fragmentation rather than process, intellectual striving and psychic unity.

H.D.'s oversweet, suffocating paradises introduced in *Sea Garden* illustrate Harold Bloom's description of the "lower paradise": "Where there is languor, the sense of the autumn of the body, there is always a suggestion of danger and limitation, particularly to the' imagination" (*Yeats* 109). Although the "I" throughout most of H.D.'s *Sea Garden* is deliberately androgynous, she/he perceives the overflowered paradise as a sensuous trap. "I have had enough / I gasp for breath," cries the speaker in "Sheltered Garden," oppressed by the stifling enclosure of "border-pinks, clove-pinks, wax-lilies, / herbs, sweet-cress // . . . border on border of scented pinks" (*CP*, 10). In poems such as "Garden" and "Orchard," the hot, overripe late-summer/autumnal paradises with their "grapes, red purple . . . dripping with wine" evoke the cloying sweetness of the lower paradise (*CP*, 29). The atmosphere of the sheltered garden, like the Venusberg, suggests stasis and torpor: "this beauty . . . without strength chokes out life"; "fruit cannot drop / through this thick air" (*CP*, 20, 25). H.D.'s speakers long to break out of their psychic paralysis and escape to the heady freedom of the alternate stormy landscape:

O to blot out this garden
to forget, to find a new beauty
in some terrible
wind-tortured place. (*CP*, 21)

The only gendered poem in *Sea Garden*, "The Gift," reveals H.D.'s association of the sheltered garden with the traditional Romantic Venusberg. In that poem H.D.'s tormented speaker suffers under the influence of a sensuous "Venus" whose garden is "oversweet . . . strangling with its myrrh-lilies" and imaginatively frees herself in a sparse, tranquil seascape (*CP*, 18).

—Cassandra Laity, "H.D's Romantic Landscapes: The Sexual Politics of the Garden." *Sagetrieb* 6:2 (Fall 1987): pp. 60–62.

EILEEN GREGORY ON H.D. AND THE GREEK ANTHOLOGY

[Eileen Gregory is the founding editor of the *H.D. Newsletter* and the author of *H.D. and Hellenism* and *Summoning the Familiar: Powers and Rites of Common Life*. In this essay, Gregory examines H.D.'s interaction with the Greek Anthology and the way in which her engagement mirrors her evolution from Imagism to revisionist myth-making.]

February 1914	"Hermonax" (Antipater of Sidon and Philodemus)
1922	"Heliodora" (Meleager)
1922	"Lais" (Plato)
1923	"Nossis" (Nossis and Meleager's poem)
	in *Heliodora*
1925	"Antipater of Sidon" ("Where, Corinth");
	later in *Palimpsest*
1926	An epigram of Moero in *Palimpsest*
1926	An epigram of Antipater of Sidon
	("I cast my lot") in *Palimpsest*
1928	An epigram of Posidippus in *Hedylus*
1928	An epigram of Asclepiades (Sikeledes)
	in *Hedylus*

This listing indicates that H.D.'s engagement with the Anthology is divided into two distinct periods. The earlier period is during 1913, the first year of her career ("Hermonax" would also have been composed in 1913). The later period is throughout the twenties, in the aftermath of the war and the breakup of her marriage. These two periods of engagement with the Anthology are sharply distinct, representing different themes and different fictions. The division here is analogous to what we have already seen within H.D.'s Sapphic intertextuality. The first is concrete and active in its engagement with the Greek text: the second is nominal, concerned not so much with the text as with the gesture of citation, The first is dedicatory, ascetic, ritualistic, choral; the second is almost entirely amatory, with some memorial epigrams focusing on loss. The first is lyric; the second is narrative (i.e., in all of the epigrams of the twenties, the translation is an italicized "inset" within a dramatic or narrative discourse).

These two periods of H.D.'s engagement with the Anthology correspond to divisions within her career that have increasingly been noted by critics, most fully by Susan Friedman: the "early H.D.," with her stringent aesthetic disciplines; and the post-1916 H.D., beginning to re-create or rewrite a fiction of herself. That transitional self-fiction of the twenties, if the Sapphic fragment poems and the later contextualized epigrams are a reliable indication, is a decidedly erotic and romantic one, though still haunted by the old athenian daimons. This later fictional H.D., like Hedylus, has "a set Dionysiac mask. . . grown uncanny" (104).

Of the considerable comment generated by H.D.'s early imagist poetry, represented in the four 1913 poems listed above, very little has been said in any detail about the relation of the poems to the Greek epigrams at their origin. Brendan Jackson makes the argument that H.D. in these poems is not an imagist because she does not obey Pound's rules of concision, but rather dilates and expands on the original. But then these poems precede Pound's dictates on imagism, and H.D. never claimed to be following such rules. Robert Babcock ("Verses" 208–12) gives an excellent, detailed reading of the least known of these Anthology poems, "Epigram / (*After the Greek*)," though he accepts Jackson's argument that concision in translation of the original is the single criterion for judging the success of the poems.

The issue to be considered here is not H.D.'s obedience to critical definitions established by others, but rather her actual practice in intertextual engagement with the Greek text, which has its own distinct character and integrity. In this regard one should note that Mackail's *Select Epigrams from the Greek Anthology* is H.D.'s bible for the Greek text and the translation of poems within the Greek Anthology. H.D.'s epithets for Sappho and for Theocritus in her essays—"little, but all roses," and "Curled Thyme"—come from Mackail's translations of epigrams, as do many of the epigrams quoted in the essays and in narratives, such as Simonides' epigram on the Spartan dead at Thermopylae. In H.D.'s engagement with the Greek Anthology, Mackail's texts stand in the same intermediary role as Wharton's Sappho.

In the three dedicatory poems, "Hermes of the Ways," "Orchard," and "Hermonax," H.D. engages the Greek texts in very much the way that she does in the opening chorus of Euripides' *Iphigeneia in Aulis.* She plays on original images—sometimes from more than one epigram—to create a visual, dimensional, tactile space. Concision of translation is certainly not the point—rather it is cosmogony. The physical location of the herm implied in an epigram by Anyte—"I, Hermes, stand here by the windy cross-ways nigh the grey sea-shore" (trans. Mackail)—becomes in "Hermes of the Ways" the sensory, whirling, vectored space of part I (west, east, front) and the more static but differentiated space of part II (stream *below* ground, poplar-shaded hill *above*, sea foaming *around*). Moreover, in each of these three poems she shifts voice and perspective to the choral "I," the one who enters the created precinct and makes an offering. Finally, in each case the poems are reflexive: the offering or sacrifice to the god is the poem itself, which reflects the god in its harsh liminality ("Hermes of the Ways") or its broken, unlovely fertility ("Orchard") or its sea strangeness ("Hermonax").

—Eileen Gregory, "H.D. and the Classical Lyric." *H.D. and Hellenism: Classical Lines* (New York: Cambridge University Press, 1997): pp.168–169.

"Fragment 113"

The poem appeared in 1921 in H.D.'s second book of poems entitled *Hymen*. The word 'hymen' has three related meanings. Originally, it stood for the marriage song of the ancient Greeks, then for the God of marriage, conceived of as an older Cupid or Eros, and finally, the means by which a bridegroom might know if his bride came to him a maiden. Indeed, this thin membrane was often referred to as the maidenhead, suggesting in its very language its importance in the characterization of women. In many ways, this poem chooses to refigure the notion of what the marriage song should be and what it should celebrate.

H.D. began the poem with one of the remaining fragments of poetry written by the 6th century lyric poet, Sappho, a writer from the Isle of Lesbos. Her poetry and her name are often associated with homoeroticism between women. "Fragment 113" was one of five Sapphic fragments re-visioned by H.D., each of which in some way tackles representations of romance and heterosexual love, often to refute those representations and the patriarchal ideals behind them. H.D. used the fragments as catalysts to create new poems rather than to translate directly; she felt particularly averse to a direct translation, thinking it a form of sacrilege, instead she chose to approach the fragment as an opportunity for exploration. What she created from "Fragment 113" was a refusal to accept typical, sentimental illusions of love, particularly of heterosexual love, rather the poem suggests and celebrates a more fiery relationship. To the mind of H.D., Sappho and her poetry represented nothing soft, but a fiercer, more real possibility for love, one that sustained and tempered itself through intensity.

The poem begins with Sappho's epigraph: "Neither honey nor bee for me." H.D. expounds on the idea, adding her own negation of popular notions of love. She will not take the sweetness of honey, for love is not sweet. She does not accept "the plunder of the bee," an image easily analogous with heterosexual intercourse. Her word choice in "plunder" also suggests unwillingness on the part of the woman as well as a commodified sexuality. Her rejection crosses geography:

from meadow or sand-flower
or mountain bush;
from winter flower or shoot
born of the later heat:

She reiterates her rejection: "not honey, not the sweet/ stain on the lips and teeth." She continues to distance herself from the supposed sweetness of this love, which moves from sweetness to "the deep/ plunge of soft belly/" an image violent and sexual, suggesting again heterosexual intercourse, focusing primarily on the polarization of the sexes. The man figures as a sort of sexual pirate and the woman figures as a "soft" sort of receptacle. H.D. further enhances that idea in the next line with an image specific to nature but evocative of a dependent mind-set for women: "and the clinging of the gold-edged/ pollen dusted feet."

In the next stanza, H.D. maintains her refusal, continuing her single sentence diatribe against romantic love. She overtly acknowledges for the first time, although the sensual language of the first stanza suggests it, the power of a romantic, sexual heterosexual love. Rapture blinds her; she tastes hunger in her mouth, "crisp/ dark and inert" an image suggesting the vaginal passage. Still, she asserts again her disinterest:

not honey, not the south;
not the tall stalk
of red twin-lilies,
nor light branch of fruit tree
caught in flexible light branch;

The tall stalk of the lilies can represent two things: in the language of flowers the lily is the coquette, a sort of frippery of which the narrator would think little. Second, the stalk may be seen as a phallic representation, red being the traditional color for eros, power and love. The narrator dismisses both ideas, and denies desire for any sort of peace represented by the fruit branch. She remains adamant. In the third stanza, the poet begins to foreshadow the true intent of her work. She does not want simply to deny romantic love; she wants to espouse a higher order of love, one not based solely in the physical or traditional representations of love.

This becomes clear in her description of the sun's relation to the iris:

for the fleck of the sun's fire,
gathers such heat and power,
that shadow-print is light,
cast through the petals
of the yellow iris flower;

Suddenly, the poet loses interest in the negation; instead, she reveres the power of the sun, which even in its smallest form, a fleck, has the power and heat to destroy, to cast shadows, to pass through something and change it. These lines rage against the flower that cannot absorb nor withstand the heat.

The poem makes its turn in the fourth and final stanza from negative to celebratory. She begins with her selection:

not iris—old desire—old passion—
old forgetfulness—old pain—
not this or any flower,

She makes her final stand against the past: no more simple sexual desire that leads to nothing, to being abandoned or forgotten. Instead, she urges:

but if you turn again,
seek strength of arm and throat,
touch as the god;
neglect the lyre-note;
knowing that you shall feel,
about the frame,
no trembling of the string
but heat, more passionate
of bone and the white shell
and fiery tempered steel.

The poet remains insistent but now that insistence is in service of a more positive belief. She persuades with fervency, counseling readers to ignore the romance of the lyre and seek power instead. Look for strength in the arm that can work, in the throat which carries the sound of intelligence and a higher passion than that of the flesh. Leave behind the easy seduction of the bloom, its fleshy attraction that so soon dies, leaving behind pain and feelings of abandonment. Look to the structure of the thing, therein lies its power. Fierce heat tempers steel, making it stronger, more resilient. Choose the intense love that will temper rather than break. Choose the white shell that encompasses the entirety of the color spectrum and purifies it. The shell provides structure and strength and most of all, remains at the most fundamental level. This version of love will last.

This single searing vision may have been an autobiographical response to the men in H.D.'s life. In 1918, H.D. found herself alone, pregnant, nearly penniless and quite ill. Both her husband and the father of her child had deserted her. The individual who supported her financially and emotionally was her close friend, Winnifred Ellerman (Bryher). The two women lived and worked together, raising H.D.'s child together. These biographical notes help to elucidate some of H.D.'s intention or, at the very least, some of her notions regarding love. Speculation as to whether their relationship was platonic or sexual varies although most agree that at one point the two women were physically intimate. Regardless, this bond may be described as Sapphic, due to the love between the two women, and this love, contrary to the love of the past, did not abandon her. It saw her through two world wars, the birth of her child and became stronger with each experience. Though it does not directly espouse homosexual love, and that seems hardly the point, the poem does question the very foundations upon which romantic, heterosexual love is grounded.

"Fragment 113"

SUSAN GUBAR ON SAPPHIC IMAGERY

[Susan Gubar is a Distinguished Professor of English and Women's Studies at Indiana University. She is the co-author of *Madwoman in the Attic: The Women Writer and the 19th Century Literary Imagination,* a runner-up for both the Pulitzer Prize and the National Book Award as well as numerous books of criticism and poetry. She has received awards from the National Endowment for Humanities and the Guggenheim Foundation. In this essay, Gubar discusses H.D.'s adoption of the intense images of Sappho as a means by which she meant avoid sentimentality.]

H.D.'s first use of Sappho, "Fragment 113," is an original poem that presents itself as an exploration of Sappho's fragment "Neither honey nor bee for me." Organized around a series of negatives, this poem refrains from assenting to an old desire. "Not honey," the poet reiterates three times in the first stanza, refusing thereby "the sweet / stain on the lips and teeth" as well as "the deep plunge of soft belly." The voluptuous flight of the plundering bee is associated with sweetness and softness. "Not so" would the poet desire, "though rapture blind my eyes, / and hunger crisp, dark and inert, my mouth." Refusing "old desire—old passion— / old forgetfulness—old pain—," H.D. speculates on a different desire:

> but if you turn again,
> seek strength of arm and throat
> touch as the god;
> neglect the lyre-note;
> knowing that you shall feel,
> about the frame,
> no trembling of the string,
> but heat, more passionate
> of bone and the white shell
> and fiery tempered steel.

Bone, not belly; shell, not lyre; fiery tempered steel instead of the stealings of the plundering bee: as in her essay on Sappho, H.D. finds in Sappho's poems "not heat in the ordinary sense, diffused and comforting," but intensity "as if the brittle crescent-moon gave heat to us, or some splendid, scintillating star turned warm suddenly in our hand like a jewel."

Sappho's imagery—the storm-tossed rose, lily, and poppy; the wind-swept sea garden; the golden Aphrodite—dominates H.D.'s early poetry. The lyricism of both poets is characterized by a yearning intensity expressed through direct address and situated in a liminal landscape. In her notes on Sappho, entitled "The Island," H.D. imagines Sappho as "the island of artistic perfection where the lover of ancient beauty (shipwrecked in the modern world) may yet find foothold and take breath and gain courage for new ventures and dream of yet unexplored continents and realms of future artistic achievement." Certainly, from H.D.'s earliest imagist verse to her later, longer epics, the Greek island is a place of female artistry. Specifically, from her dramatization in "Callypso" of Odysseus fleeing Calypso's island, to her paradisal vision in *Trilogy* of "the circles and circles of islands / about the lost center-island, Atlantis," to the central section of *Helen in Egypt*, which is situated on Leuke, *l'île blanche*, H.D. affirms what she proclaims in her last volume, *Hermetic Definition*, that "the island is herself, is her."

Susan Friedman has explained that "Sappho's influence on imagists no doubt helped to validate H.D.'s leadership role in the development of the modern lyric." Just as important, Sappho's Greek fragments furnished H.D. a linguistic model for the poems that would define the imagist aesthetic. "Fragment 113" presents itself as a numbered remnant, a belated version of a mutilated vision, a translation of a lost original. As H.D. knew, Sappho's texts, excavated in 1898 from Egyptian debris, survived as narrow strips torn from mummy wrappings. Her own poems, narrow columns of print with not a few phrases broken off with dashes, meditate on a loss they mediate as the speaker's series of negatives, presumably a response to a prior sentence omitted from the poem, seem to imply that the text has been torn out of an unrecoverable narrative context. H.D.'s lifelong effort to recreate what has been "scattered in the shards / men tread upon" is reflected in her early fascination with Sappho's poetry, as is her recurrent presentation of herself as a translator of unearthed texts that can never, be fully restored or understood. Certainly, H.D. uses the runes of Sappho as the fragments she shores up against her own ruin.

"Fragment 113" was published in the volume *Hymen* in 1921. Significantly, in the title piece of this volume, H.D. begins to extend her short lyrics in the direction of narrative. A cluster of poems describes the bride's impending fate, the loss of her virginity, in terms of the plundering bee who "slips / Between the purple flower-lips." In the context of Sappho's "Neither honey nor bee for me," H.D.'s image of the bee's penetration brings to the foreground the silence and isolation of the veiled, white figure of the bride. In addition, as Alicia Ostriker has pointed out, the very title, "Hymen," with its evocation both of female anatomy and of a male god, turns this celebratory sequence into a somber meditation on the predatory pattern of heterosexuality, a pattern explicitly associated with the simultaneity of the bride's marriage and her divorce from the female community. H.D. transforms Sappho's epithalamia into the choruses of girls, maidens, matrons, and priestesses accompanying the silent bride. The stage directions between the lyrics consist of descriptions of musical interludes (flute, harp), of costumes (tunics, baskets), and of the spatial arrangement of figures in their processionals before the temple of Hera. Linking the lyrics together into a liturgy, these italicized prose passages solve the poetic problem H.D. faced as she struggled to extend a minimalist form without losing the intensity she associated with the image. "Hymen" therefore epitomizes the way in which Sappho empowered H.D. to turn eventually toward a reinvention of Homeric epic in *Helen in Egypt*, where she perfected the interrelationships between individual lyrics and a prose gloss that contextualizes them.

> —Susan Gubar, "Sapphistries." *Signs* 10:1 (Autumn 1984): pp. 53–56.

DONNA KROLIK HOLLENBERG ON THE 'WHITE STATE' IN H.D.'S POETRY

[Donna Krolik Hollenberg is an Associate Professor of English at University of Connecticut. She has published three books on H.D. Here, she investigates the white state of creativity as a rebellion against heterosexual love and a restoration of female autonomy in the poem, particularly as it fits in with a larger group of poems from the poet's early Imagistic work in *Hymen*.]

An alternative, "white" emotional state, linked with restored integrity and lesbian love, informs a second important group of poems in *Hymen*: "White World," "Prayer," "Song," "Evadne," "The Islands," "At Baia," "Fragment 113," and "Egypt." "The whole white world is ours," H.D. writes in the first section of this group, and "delight / waits till our spirits tire / of forest, grove and bush / and purple flower of the laurel tree" (*CP*, 134). "Prayer," "Song," and "Evadne" develop nuances of this white world. As in her unpublished novel *Paint It Today*, H.D. associates whiteness with intactness, with the chaste terms of artistic inspiration, and with creation divorced from procreation. For example, the prayer to Athene asks that the goddess touch the speaker's forehead, thus restoring "glamour to our will, / the thought . . . the tool, the chisel" (*CP*, 142). "Song" personifies its subject as a rarefied fertility god or goddess, whose face is as "fair as rain, / yet as rain that lies clear / on white honey-comb" (*CP*, 133). And Evadne, united with Apollo, claims that "Between my chin and throat / his mouth slipped over and over" (*CP*, 132).

Similarly, "The Islands" and "At Baia" celebrate an inviolate artistic integrity. The former answers the question "What are the islands to me," with a luxurious catalogue of Greek place-names so euphonious and beautifully paced they should be set to music. The question is subtly complicated in the poem's seven sections to develop a finely honed contrast: "What can love of land give to me / that you have not?" (*CP*, 125). It finally comes to rest, unanswered, upon the "cold splendour of song / and its bleak sacrifice" (*CP*, 127). At Baia, the ancient port of Cumae, which is inseparably associated with the Sybil, the speaker meditates on the salutary gift of oracular expression. By elaborating on a comparison with "some lovely, perilous thing, / orchids piled in a great sheaf," she implies the ineffable, metaphysical fragrance she seeks: "Lover to lover, no kiss, / no touch, but forever and ever this" (*CP*, 128).

H.D. connects this alternative, "white," emotional state more explicitly with lesbian love in "Fragment 113" and "Egypt." In the former poem she dilates Sappho's "Neither honey nor bee for me" into an ingeniously wrought comparison between degrees and modes of passion. Throughout half of the poem the speaker's reiterated denials ring subtle changes upon the "old" sensual "plunder" she refuses because it has caused her to suffer:

> not honey, not the south;
>
> . . .
>
> not iris—old desire—old passion
> old forgetfulness—old pain—
> not this, nor any flower. (*CP*, 131)

Finally, she admonishes the other to "touch as the god," to "seek strength of arm and throat," to prefer intellectual love, the lyre's "fiery-tempered" frame to the trembling lyre note.

> —Donna Krolik Hollenberg, "H.D.'s Imagery: A Poetry of Loss and Rebellion." *H.D." The Poetics of Childbirth and Creativity* (Boston: Northeastern University Press, 1991): pp. 82–84.

HELEN SWORD ON LOVE AND THE SELF

> [Helen Sword is an Associate Professor of English at Indiana University and an Adjunct Associate Professor in Comparative Literature. She is the author of *Engendering Inspiration: Visionary Strategies in Rilke, Lawrence and H.D.* Here, she uses the fragment poems to discuss H.D.'s fear of heterosexual love as a process of possessing through which identity is lost.]

The poems of *Hymen* and *Heliodora*, published in the early 1920s, explore in often harrowing detail the workings of the divine madness provoked, according to Socrates' schema, by Eros and Aphrodite. Neither volume, to be sure, focuses exclusively on the negative aspects of erotic desire: some poems, such as "Evadne," cheerfully celebrate sexual love (*CP*, 132); others, such as "Hymen" and "Leda," associate marriage and sexuality with a measured, abstract grace (101–10, 120–21); and others still, such as "Lethe" and the Sapphic "Fragment 113," reject sexuality (or at least heterosexuality) altogether: "Neither honey nor bee for me" (131, 190). The majority of these poems, however, persistently enact situations of emotional manipulation and entrapment, reflecting the poet's wary conviction that possession, whether of the divine or the sexual kind, can lead to a frightening, debilitating loss of self.

Throughout both volumes H.D. not only celebrates powerful goddesses such as Artemis and Demeter but also lends her voice to such abused, abandoned, and silenced women from the past as Iphigenia, Eurydice, Ariadne, and Penelope. In addition, she rehabilitates a number of women traditionally regarded as evil temptresses—figures such as Phaedra, Helen, and Circe—by showing that they, too, have in their own ways been victims of divine and human machinations. Only Aphrodite, perpetrator of the erotic madness that claims throughout H.D.'s work so many tragic victims, receives no such redemptive treatment. Instead, H.D.'s poetic relationship with the goddess of love is characterized by a profound ambivalence, as she tries to reconcile the agony of unrequited passion and the bitterness of loss with the creativity and joy sparked by erotic desire.

This vexed stance toward Aphrodite is perhaps most explicitly enacted in a series of verses loosely based on fragments from Sappho, patroness of love poets and particularly of female poets. For instance, in "Fragment Forty-one" (". . . thou flittest to Andromeda"), the poet insists that, although Aphrodite has tortured her by allowing her lover to fall in love with another woman, she herself has always remained a faithful devotee of the goddess:

> I too have followed
> her path.
> I too have bent at her feet.
> (*CP*, 181)

In "Fragment Sixty-eight" (". . . even in the house of Hades"), similarly, the poet continues to honor Aphrodite even though she has been "trapped" and "slain" by her:

> though I break,
> crushed under the goddess' hate,
> though I fall beaten at last,
> so high have I thrust my glance
> up into her presence.
> (189)

While she does not exempt from blame the lover who has deserted her—"What can death mar in me / that you have not?" (188)—she implies that Aphrodite, above all, is responsible for her pain: the poet has been victimized as much by the vindictive goddess who plagues her with erotic desire as by the mortal man who has rejected her. H.D.'s tendency to blame love rather than the lover bears out Adrienne Rich's assertion that female poets seldom protest male oppression directly:

> Until recently this female anger and this furious awareness of the Man's power over her were not available materials to the female poet, who tended to write of Love as the source of her suffering, and to view that victimization by Love as an almost inevitable fate. Or, like Marianne Moore and Elizabeth Bishop, she kept sexuality at a measured and chiseled distance in her poems. ("When We Dead Awaken: Writing as Re-Vision," *On Lies* 36).

Indeed, by placing a female in the role of rapist—Aphrodite, after all, violates the poet's peace of mind, if not her body—H.D. suggests, problematically, that the anguished love poet is the victim less of an invasive, external Other than of an internalized, female destructive force. As in "Mid-day," then, in which "my thoughts" and "I" become separate and antagonistic entities, the poet, tortured by her own emotions and desires, becomes possessed, in a sense, by herself.

"Fragment Forty" ("Love . . . bitter-sweet") offers one explanation why the poet, despite the pain that erotic desire has caused her, continues to worship at the shrine of love, which is both "bitter" and "sweet," both "honey" and "salt" (*CP*, 173). Love here is personified not by Aphrodite but, instead, by her son Eros, a capricious and elusive god; the poem addresses the impossibility of imprisoning him or, by extension, of sustaining any form of romantic love for long. In a series of comparisons recalling the flower and sea imagery of *Sea Garden*, the poet admits her astonishment that her lover's unfaithfulness, a manifestation of Eros's cruelty and power, has not crushed and destroyed her:

> I had thought myself frail;
> a petal,
> with light equal
> on leaf and under-leaf.

I had thought myself frail;
a lamp,
shell, ivory or crust of pearl,
about to fall shattered,
with flame spent.
                    (174–75)

As in *Sea Garden*, however, the very force that threatens to annihi-
late the poet actually lends her strength: "to sing love," she coura-
geously asserts, "love must first shatter us" (175). To some extent, of
course, the poet's determination to put a brave face on the matter
smacks of pure survivalism: having been both "deserted" and "shattered" by love, she seeks to make the best of her pain, transforming
bitterness into sweetness, bitter experience into art. On the other
hand, however, the conclusion of "Fragment Forty" reflects a very
real belief on H.D.'s part—one shared, as I have shown, by precur-
sors including Goethe and Blake as well as by Rilke and
Lawrence—that adversity and contradiction are necessary precondi-
tions for creativity. Forcefully demonstrating that erotic madness
need not necessarily lead to a loss of self-control and thence to self-
destruction, H.D. shows instead that possession begets self-posses-
sion: just as she can craft well-wrought poems from Sapphic fragments, so she can forge art from agony, triumph from despair.

—Helen Sword, "H.D. and the Poetics of Possession." *Engendering
Inspiration: Visionary Strategies in Rilke, Lawrence and H.D.* (Ann
Arbor: University of Michigan, 1995): pp. 127–129

EILEEN GREGORY ON THE FUNCTION OF SAPPHO

[In this extract Gregory examines H.D.'s ambiguous use of
Sappho, citing the poet's refusal to translate or to engage
new translations of her poems despite her obvious textual
connections.]

One must take seriously H.D.'s claim to "superstition"; her relation
to Sappho would seem indeed to be implicated in an irrational and
ominous sense of taboo. Why else would an ambitious poet-translator

and committed hellenic revolutionary to whom Sappho is a pivotal figure deliberately refuse a direct textual encounter, insisting rather on literary mediation and on a limited and thoroughly naturalized body of fragments? Unlike her male predecessors and peers, and indeed unlike female predecessors such as Michael Field and René Vivien," H.D. chooses to abstain completely from public intercourse with the textual body of the Mitylenean.

H.D.'s literary relation to Sappho, then, would seem to possess this intricate dynamic: she overtly embraces Sappho as a precursor in the fragment poems and the essays, but at the same time avoids her as a translator and scholar; and all the while, as seems clear from the catalogue in the Appendix, she works out a covert textual exchange in her own terms. This assertion may seem excessively subtle. However, critics have come to similar conclusions about H.D.'s circuitous appropriation of male figures in her life, such as Lawrence, Pound, and Freud. Further, this stance toward Sappho reflects to some extent the hesitations of other modern women writers who discover the "liabilities of such a collaboration" (Gubar 47). But a crucial aspect of this puzzle lies in Sappho's centrality within fictions of maternal desire in H.D.'s writing. The fear of sacrilege surrounding the sacred text of Sappho may imply for H.D. that her words are not only untranslatable, but "unspeakable," in the sense that Deborah Kelly Kloepfer has amplified, associated with a "maternally connoted homoeroticism" (122). They are *ta arreta*, things interdicted, like the Eleusinian mysteries; and indeed Sappho, at least in some of H.D.'s writing, seems fairly clearly implicated in an Eleusinian territory.

Within H.D.'s intricate Sapphic intertextuality, one may distinguish between an overt and a covert interplay, the former evident in the fragment poems, the latter in some of the other early lyrics, especially the poems of "Hymen." Because the fragment poems have received substantial comment, I treat them here only briefly and somewhat generally, in an attempt to define their place within H.D.'s fictions of Sappho.

A quotation of a Sapphic fragment in the Wharton translation appears as the title or subtitle of six poems. Five name the number from Wharton, who follows the edition of Theodor Bergk (113, 36, 40, 41, and 68); and one, "Calliope," gives a fragment as a subtitle without a number. A seventh of these fragment poems—"Choros Sequence / from *Morpheus*"—quotes a fragment as a subtitle without appending Sappho's name. H.D.'s textual relation to Sappho in these poems is more complex than critics have granted. What precisely does it signify to entitle a poem, for instance, "Fragment 113 / `Neither honey nor bee for me*—Sappho"? The title insists on textuality—Sappho represented as a textual fragment, within a numbered sequence of fragments, within a specific edition (Bergk) and a specific translation (Wharton). But at the same time the poem flamboyantly denies or resists that specific textuality in a free extrapolation, in which the original phrase is often repeated, altered, played out, quizzed, turned, to the point that its frail simple sense, much less its contextualized sense, is effectively dissolved. In "Fragment 113," the phrase "Neither honey nor bee for me" becomes a digressive, extenuated series of voluptuous denials of voluptuousness, leading to a rhetorical turn in affirming the dialectical opposite, a hard, skeletal asceticism.

The many-times-removed text of Sappho has indeed a spectral presence here. Where, how, and what is "Sappho" in these poems? The cited fragment, I would suggest, is not as important as the gesture of citation. The purpose clearly is not interpretation or representation, but rather invocation. "Sappho" stands as a sign announcing a certain conscribed and determined musing on states of passion. Each of these seven poems, regardless of the dramatic situation framing it, explores rhetorically a particular erotic crux or impasse. Erotic tension—or a kind of debate within the laws of love—is what all the poems have in common: tension or debate between sensual and ascetic possession and rapture ("Fragment 113"); between "song's gift" or "love's gift," vocation or sexual passion ("Fragment Thirty-six"); between spirit and flesh ("Calliope"); between love as sweet and as bitter ("Fragment Forty"); between the rancor of jealousy and the love of love ("Fragment Forty-one"); between desire for a betraying lover's presence and desire for death ("Fragment Sixty-eight"); and between Dionysian heat and oblivion and Apollonian cold and clarity ("Choros Sequence / from *Morpheus*"). Though certainly this summary does not communicate the complexity of the poems, it nevertheless makes clear that each of them turns rhetorically on the device of antithesis and that each engages a version of the oppositions central to H.D.'s fictions of divine mania.

"Sappho" in these poems is a marker, signaling a certain kind of imaginative engagement, even a certain literary *topos*. Longinus in his essay on the sublime praises above all Sappho's ability to express the oppositions and contradictions within erotic madness (*erotika mania*). Her poems express "not one single emotion but a concourse of emotions" (trans. Campbell 1:81)—the *concordia discors* that is the stock-in-trade of subsequent lyricists. Longinus then cites, and thus preserves, an example, "He is like a god to me, the man who sits beside you" (*LP*, 31), a poem describing in detail the phenomenon of erotic seizure, likening it to the physical experience of dying. In part because of the preservation of this poem and commentary, Sappho has been traditionally seen as *the* consummate poet of eros, specifically, of erotic crisis.

By the time that H.D. engages this literary fiction, Sappho carries the cumulative weight of Western love theology, prominently the iconography of troubadour passion. Swinburne calls her "Love's priestess, mad with pain and joy of song, / Song's priestess, mad with joy and pain of love" ("On the Cliffs" 3:317). The aesthetic/decadent glamour of Sappho as a literary sign thus links religion, love, song, madness, pain, and joy. In late-nineteenth-century commentaries it was common to associate Sappho with the troubadours, as one who like them knows the dominion of Love or "overmastering emotion" (Symonds 1:293). In an extended comparison of Sappho as lyricist with the Provençal poets, J. M. Mackail says, "The Love whom she saw . . . 'descending from heaven clad in purple vesture,' is akin to the intellectual and spiritual love of Plato and of Dante" (*Lectures* 107). Like Dante she represents an openness to "Love terrible with banners." H.D. and her generation, inheriting the emphases of aesthetic hellenism, certainly knew of these associations: Pound in his early *The Spirit of Romance* finds Sappho in Arnaut Daniel and Dante (93, 122). She clearly possesses an iconic role in what H.D. and Pound, along with late-nineteenth-century hellenists, considered the main line of lyric development from the Greeks through the early Renaissance.

H.D. herself acknowledges this allegorical status of the figure: "Sappho has become for us a name, an abstraction as well as a pseudonym for poignant human feeling" ("The Wise Sappho" 67). The "Sappho" of the fragment poems, I would suggest, is this verbal icon, abstraction, "pseudonym," or metonym—a mark of magical glamour. She is in Swinburne's phrase "Our Lady of all men's loves" ("On the Cliffs" 3:322), and like the Lady of the troubadours, as Pound claims, she functions as a mantra focusing the creative energies of the poet.

—Eileen Gregory, "H.D. and the Classical Lyric." *H.D. and Hellenism* (New York: Cambridge University Press, 1997): pp. 151–153.

DIANA COLLECOTT ON THE POEMS AS DRAMATIC LYRICS

[Diana Collecott is founding co-editor of The Basil Bunting Poetry Centre as well as a Senior Fulbright Scholar. In this essay, she posits H.D.'s dramatic lyrics, particularly her Sapphic fragments, as representative of a movement away from the limits of Imagism.]

Seeking a way out of Imagisme, she began to incorporate the codes of other genres in her poetic writing. Here too she followed Stesichorus, who was renowned for his synthesis of lyric verse, dramatic chorus and heroic narrative. In modern poetry, the narrative code of telling a story and the dramatic code of speaking in character come together most persuasively in the dramatic monologue. Robert Browning, who described his *Dramatic Lyrics* as 'so many utterances of imaginary persons, not mine', used the genre as an explicit alternative to the romantic confessional style. H.D. was well aware of this precursor and, using his preferred term, described the 'dramatic lyric' as 'the most difficult form in the language' ('Farmer's'). In dramatic monologues such as 'Piere Vidal Old' and 'Gerontion', Pound and Eliot took Browning and Tennyson as their models: H.D. had an earlier model in Sappho. As we saw in chapter I, though often treated as confessional, Sappho's compositions are just as likely to have been dramatic lyrics. Moreover, when H.D. composed her variations on Sapphic fragments, she created complex soliloquies for 'imaginary persons' for whom Sappho's words form dramatic masks. Thus 'Fragment 113' ("*Neither honey nor bee for me*") is spoken by one who believes s/he will no more love or be

loved, while 'Fragment Forty-one' (`. . . *thou flittest to Andromeda*')
is spoken by one whom a lover has betrayed.

H.D.'s use of fictive and mythic characters allowed her to develop the dramatic lyric even in her earliest work. Consequently, her poetic innovations include not only Imagist techniques of sensory presentation, but also non-Imagist techniques of vocalisation. These experiments in both modes coincided with her most intensive period of translation from classical Greek drama, between 1913 (when she started work on Euripides' *Iphigenia in Aulis* and *Hippolytus*) and 1927 (when she published her own verse drama, *Hippolytus Temporizes*). The 'masque' of *Hymen* reflects this apprenticeship, as do the individual poems in that volume and in *Heliodora*. Their titles identify a *dramatis personae* of goddesses, heroines and mortal women: Demeter, Thetis, Circe, Helen, Cassandra, Leda, Evadne, Phaedra. Although these recall ancient myth, they allow a modern woman to combine the Imagist requirement of 'direct treatment of the "thing" (whether subjective or objective)' with the 'indirect method' of dramatic characterisation.

In a circular of 1912, *Poetry* promised to consider 'All kinds of verse . . . *narrative, dramatic, lyric*'; the magazine's original policy, before Pound's pressure on it to promote Imagisme, was 'to print poems of greater length . . . than the other magazines can afford to use'. H.D.'s experiments, even while she was being published as the exemplary Imagist, were consonant with this initiative: Glenn Hughes would notice, between 1914 and 1931, her development towards longer poems. Pound, however, created Vorticism to sustain the compression of 'Imagisme', which he distinguished sharply from 'lyric' ('Vorticism' 82–3). At the same time, H.D. frequently combined lyric, drama and narrative in a single speaking voice. For instance, 'Loss' is spoken by the survivor of a disastrous battle fought at the edge of the sea who is nonetheless glad that a beloved companion has escaped defeat and torture by drowning:

> I am glad the tide swept you out,
> O beloved,
> you of all this ghastly host
> alone untouched,
> your white flesh covered with salt
> as with myrrh and burnt iris. (*Collected* 22)

'Loss' was one of the poems in *Sea Garden* best loved by Bryher, who declared that she knew that book by heart before meeting its author (*Heart* 187); it also shows H.D. beginning to investigate homosexual love. In 'Loss', as later in 'I Said'/'To W.B.', this process involves the impersonation of a speaking subject whose gender is never revealed, with an intense eroticism and without any of the 'sentimentalism' that Marsden ascribed to the love poets or the past. *Sea Garden* is characterised by poems such as 'Mid-day', and 'Sheltered Garden', which consist of emotions expressed in the first person singular. So much so that a narrative can be elicited from sequences of statements like these: '*I am startled . . . I am anguished. . . I dread . . . I perish*'; 'I have had enough. I gasp for breath' (*Collected* 10, 19). The palpable presence of a speaker distinguishes poems of this kind from the poetic proposed by Pound in 'A Few Don'ts by an Imagiste'.

—Diana Collecott, 'the art of the future:' Her Emergence from Imagism." *H.D. and Sapphic Modernism* (Cambridge: Cambridge University Press, 1999): pp. 154–155.

"Helen"

With the 1924 publication of *Heliodora*, H.D. introduced her first re-visioning of Helen of Troy, a figure who would haunt her poems and parallel the author's own evolution both as a writer and a woman. Influenced by Euripides's sympathetic portrayal of Helen, H.D. relies heavily on the reader's associations with Greco-Roman history in this three-stanza poem. In Greek myth, Helen is said to be the product of a union between Zeus, who disguised himself as a swan, and Leda, the mortal woman he raped. The consummation spawned four children, who hatched from eggs, one of whom being Helen. Upon entering adolescence, Helen became the most beautiful woman in Greece, coveted by all. This beauty brought ceaseless disaster. Theseus, king of Athens, kidnapped Helen, to fulfill his wish to have sex with one of Zeus's daughters before he died. After accomplishing his goal, he left Helen behind as he pursued other adventures. During his absence, Helen's brothers found her and returned her to Sparta where the decision was made that Helen should marry. Suitors flocked to the kingdom, a veritable who's who of Greek society. In order to avoid negative repercussions for all concerned, Odysseus suggested that the rejected suitors take an oath to fight for the bridegroom and his marriage should anything seek to compromise it. The suitors agreed and Tyndacarus, Helen's father, selected Menelaus, brother of Agamemnon, to become the bridegroom. The marriage was politically advantageous. They married and Helen gave birth to several children. After a trip to Troy, Menaleus returned home with Paris, prince of Troy. After several days, Menaleus left the kingdom to attend a family funeral. Paris and Helen were left together and sailed for Troy soon thereafter.

Stories begin to differ here. Many claim that Helen made the decision to while others assert that Aphrodite worked to help Paris in his task of claiming her. The latter support their claim with an earlier myth wherein Paris judged a beauty contest among the goddesses, declaring Aphrodite most fair and in return, winning himself the hand of the most beautiful woman. Little did he know that woman would be Helen. Another myth claims that Aphrodite cursed Tyndacarus to have adulteress daughters. Regardless, the pair left for Troy where they married. Meanwhile, couriers scurried across the countryside to warn Menelaus, who left for Troy to negotiate her return. Paris refused to negotiate, and Menelaus retired to Sparta to prepare for war. All the former suitors were reminded of their oath to protect the marriage and joined in the fight to reclaim Helen. The Trojan War ensued, bringing with it, ten years of bloodshed and the loss of countless lives.

H.D. chooses to start her poem in the aftermath of the war. She declares "All Greece hates/" ending her line quite deliberately to indicate the absolute totality of the emotion felt by the entire populace. She is a woman utterly alone. Greece stands not as a series of city-states but as a totality, a group united in its hatred, a populace who believed in the beauty of this one woman as a valid cause for fighting. H.D. continues to give the vision of Helen, careful initially to see her as the populace saw her, as a body, an exquisite being for whom so many had died. She continues her description of the statue-like beauty:

> the still eyes in the white face
> the lustre as of olives
> where she stands,
> and the white hands.

H.D. creates a woman of almost absolute inertia. Her eyes have lustre but no movement, suggesting that her loveliness is acted upon as opposed to acting. Also, she uses the word 'white' twice, suggesting the innocence of Helen, the notion that the blood of the masses does not darken her skin. Instead, it suggests her absolution and her purity of intent, though to the eyes of Greece, it may also symbolize the distance between Helen and the destruction she caused, a distance clearly resented by the people. This layering of meaning and perspective typifies H.D.'s poetry as does the refiguring of myth.

In the next stanza, H.D. again begins with the emotional state of the populace: "All Greece reviles/." Again she ends the line abruptly, indicating the absolutism of the emotion. Despite her beauty and her purification as described in the prior stanza, she will not be forgiven for her presumed misconduct. Conveniently, or perhaps as a result of the patriarchal culture, the people forget that Helen did not choose her husband and if the myth regarding Paris is true, she did not choose him as a husband either. As from her birth, both the gods and her father decided the fate of Helen. Still, Greece reviles her:

> the wan face when she smiles,
> hating it deeper still
> when it grows wan and white,
> remembering past enchantments
> and past ills.

Suddenly, Helen ages; the beauty once thought worthy of war has lost her lovely color and allure; she slowly expires under the weight of the blame and hatred being thrust upon her. The last link to being loved is now lost. She betrayed the people by going to Troy; she betrayed them by losing her beauty. As a woman, she now possesses little value, certainly not enough for which one might fight and lose a life. She becomes a remnant of a lost war and a lost cause, better forgotten.

In the final stanza, Greece remains "unmoved" by the wan figure of Helen. H.D. refers to Helen as "God's daughter, born of love/" playing with punctuation to indicate the breadth of hypocrisy surrounding stories of Helen. Clearly, Zeus fathered Helen, but in standard written English, Greek gods are not afforded the respect of capitalization; that right belongs to the Judeo-Christian God. By the mere act of capitalization, H.D. also implicates the retellings sprung from the Western tradition which alternate between making Helen a whore or a pawn, though she is, as everyone is, God's child and worthy of his judgement alone. Both mythologies deny her any sort of autonomy and both patriarchal systems judge her and find her wanting. In either case, as God's daughter, she still elicits no sympathy. Though she was born of love, no love shall be hers. Though her body still possesses some beauty, the only way that she can be loved again is to make herself a martyr, to die. Only through a purification of death via fire will she be made pure enough to be embraced by the people, "only if she were laid, / white ash amid funeral cypresses." Death gives the people a memory that surpasses the reality and makes an unreasonable war reasonable. It provides a certain national amnesty. With Helen alive and faded, the legendary beauty stands in question, as does the motivation to war. A dead beauty wields more power than a live beauty.

The passive voice indicates that the decision to die will not be hers. H.D. posits Helen as a victim here, of circumstance, of fate, of the patriarchal culture that silenced and bound her. As a precursor to her later poem, *Helen in Egypt*, this initial vision shows the effect of the patriarchy on the position of women; in her later incarnation, Helen moves beyond the wealth of Western versions of her story and chooses to re-vision an independent existence based on a little known and little credited myth. Clearly, this early poem left Helen without recourse to save herself or her reputation. It rendered her inert, a victim of the populace, serving as a sort of introduction to the problem of woman as a public figure, a problem with which H.D. contended for most of her professional life.

"Helen"

SUSAN STANFORD FRIEDMAN ON MUTING EFFECTS

[Susan Stanford Friedman is the Virginia Woolf Professor of English and Women's Studies at the University of Wisconsin-Madison. She is the author of *Mappings: Feminism and the Cultural Geographies of Encounter* as well as two books on H.D. In this essay, she discusses the muting effect of traditional patriarchal views on the voice of Helen.]

H.D.'s "revolutionary" re-vision of tradition did not spring into being full-grown with the publication of the *Trilogy*. Instead, it was rooted firmly in her imagist poetry and grew slowly as her early fascination with mythology deepened into the religious researches of her later years. Representing different decades of her poetic career, four poems centering on goddess figures can serve as a paradigm of the growing dialectic in H.D.'s use of traditional materials: "Helen" (1923), "Callypso Speaks" (1938), *Trilogy*, and *Helen in Egypt*. They clarify not only the process of transformation, but also the progression of a gradually developing imperative to create a new mythology for women as a group.

"Helen" takes as its subject the woman who has been the literary and mythic symbol of sexual beauty and illicit love in western culture. Much has been written about her, but H.D.'s poem does something new: it implicitly attacks the traditional imagery of Helen and implies that such perspectives have silenced Helen's own voice.

> All Greece hates
> the still eyes in the white face,
> the lustre as of olives
> where she stands,
> and the white hands.

> all Greece reviles
> the wan face when she smiles,
> hating it deeper still

when it grows wan and white,
remembering past enchantments
and past ills.

Greece sees, unmoved,
God's daughter, born of love,
the beauty of cool feet
and slenderest knees,
could love indeed the maid,
only if she were laid,
white ash amid funereal cypresses. (*S.P.*, p. 48)

Like Edgar Allan Poe's poem about Helen, this poem draws a portrait with careful references to Helen's eyes, face, hands, feet, and knees. But in contrast to Poe's poem, H.D.'s Helen does not stand alone, unveiled before the adoring eyes of the male poet. Instead, she is accompanied by a hate-filled gaze that never leaves the beauty of her body. H.D.'s poem operates on an opposition established between Helen and "all Greece," and the speaker stands outside this opposition to record the interaction between the two. Time, space, and situation are left uncertain with a sparse setting that presents an image rather than a realistic event. The action verbs outline the image: Helen "stands," "smiles" faintly, and grows more "wan and white" while "all Greece" regards first her face and then "sees . . . the beauty of cool feet / and slenderest knees."

The process the speaker watches is the growing hatred of Helen and the overwhelming effect it has upon her. The emotion directed in judgment against Helen is intense—we are aware of this not only because the verbs "hates" and "reviles" stand out so starkly, but also because the impersonality of "all Greece" generalizes the condemnation. In Poe's poem, he alone worships Helen. In W. B. Yeats's "No Second Troy," the poet's feelings for Helen are more ambivalent, but Yeats still records a private experience between himself and his mythic mask for Maude Gonne. In her poem, however, H.D. generalizes those who regard Helen until they take on the dimensions of a collective culture. "Greece" is a country, not a person, not even a people. H.D.'s choice of "Greece" in place of the more logical "Greeks" suggests that the entire weight of a cultural tradition "reviles" Helen. The structural repetition of "all" at the beginning of the first two stanzas reinforces the image of a whole culture set in powerful opposition to one woman. And the lack of a realistic setting in this portrait of "all Greece" regarding Helen underlines the real subject of the poem: woman's place in male-dominated tradition.

Helen's response to the hate-filled gaze of "all Greece" is not a static one. In fact, the stanzas of the poem subtly suggest the transformation of a living woman into a marble statue, a progression from life to death controlled by the force of hate. In the first stanza, Helen seems immobilized—her eyes are "still" and she simply "stands." The emphasis on the whiteness of her face and hands adds to this image of impassivity. But, read in the light of the last two stanzas, Helen in the first stanza still has the glow of life. The poet sees the rich "lustre as of olives / where she stands." This lustre begins to disappear in the second stanza. White hands and white face are conventional attributes of female beauty. But in the second stanza, white skin "grows wan and white" in the face of increasing hatred—that is, pale, bloodless, and seemingly lifeless. As if to appease "all Greece," her "wan face . . . smiles." According to some scholars, women have traditionally relied on a perpetual smile to render themselves more acceptable in an androcentric culture. Helen too smiles in a desperate attempt to counteract the condemnation that is growing "deeper still" for her part in the Trojan War.

In the third stanza, "white" signals the final result of Greece's unmoving hatred, becoming the color of death: "white ash amid funereal cypresses." The word "unmoved" to describe a lack of compassion is something of a pun (un-moving) that echoes in reverse the increasing immobility of Helen. Her smiles win her no mercy, and the only way she can become loved is through her death. The opening image of Helen surrounded by the "lustre" of life yields to the conditional fantasy of her death, a progression underlined by the change in trees from olive to "funereal cypresses." Her feet are "Cool," not warm with life. The death imagery, however, has another dimension of meaning in Helen's relationship to tradition. As the poem records the change in Helen's reactions, it presents a dynamic image of Helen's metamorphosis into a white marble statue adored for the beauty of her "cool feet / and slenderest knees." Poe's poem ends with his vision of Helen "in yon brilliant window-niche / How statue-like I see thee stand." H.D. doesn't use the word "statue," but the central image of Helen standing before the gaze of "all Greece" suggests it. The poet watches the process of Helen's canonization as "God's daughter, born of love." The growing whiteness of her skin signals her death as a living woman and her birth as a statue, a symbol of beauty in the eyes of "all Greece."

In Poe's poem, Helen's appearance as a statue is an affirmation. But in H.D.'s poem, the speaker understands the connection between the traditional worship of woman as symbol and the death of the living woman. H.D.'s poem about Helen is a re-vision of the Medusa myth and an implicit attack on the processes of masculine myth-making with female symbols. According to Greek myth, a man's direct sight of the fearful Medusa with her hair of snakes would turn him to stone. In his famous interpretation of this myth, Freud argued that Medusa's head represented the castrated state of female genitals, and the myth embodied castration anxiety. But in H.D.'s reversal of psychoanalysis and myth, the hatred of a collective male tradition turns woman to stone, literally a statue. An added complexity, however, is that hatred becomes love once Helen's paralysis is complete. Like Joan of Arc, Helen, immobilized and silenced, is an object of worship. Alive, she was an object of hatred, a threat to the dominant culture ruled by men. As statue or symbol, she is safely controlled by the tradition that defines her through its art. What seems to be an adoration of woman, H.D. says, is rooted in reality in a hatred for the living woman who has the capacity to speak for herself.

In "Helen," the poet cannot free Helen from the patriarchal cage of traditional hate and adoration. She stands outside the process, helpless to prevent Helen's growing silence and paralysis. She can and does attack tradition, but she cannot give the mute statue a voice.

—Susan Stanford Friedman, "'Born of One Mother': Re-Vision of Patriarchal Tradition." *Psyche Reborn: The Emergence of H.D.* (Bloomington: Indiana University Press, 1981): pp. 233–235.

DONNA COPELAND ON HELEN AS A SYMBOL OF GREECE

[Here, Copeland describes Helen as a composite of the emotions and values of the Greek people, so that she becomes representative of the entire country.]

Composed of only three stanzas, the poem is a study in contrasts. The first line of the first stanza, "All Greece hates," sets the tone for the rest of the poem about the country's reaction to Helen at the end of the war with Troy. The first line of the second stanza, "All Greece reviles," and of the final stanza, "Greece sees, unmoved," paint a picture of a people whose hatred and revulsion are cold and unforgiving. As long as Helen lives, she is a painful reminder of what has been lost, and the people refuse to feel sympathy or engage their emotions until she is gone from their sight. But their hatred is not a hot passion for the fire of revenge. She can be forgiven when the purification is complete—when her white face and white hands have cooled to white ash with the passage of time.

It would seem, then, that "the still eyes in the white face . . . and the white hands" are describing a woman whom they perceive as pallid and colorless, perhaps with shame. Yet her beauty creeps into a description that strives to be emotionless. In the first stanza, "the lustre as of olives / where she stands," provides an image that contrasts with the war and the hatred expressed in the first line. Lustre suggests not only a shining or reflected light, but also glory or great fame. And, of course, the olive is a symbol of peace as well as a fruit emblematic of Greece.

In the second stanza, one line longer than the first, the description of Helen is expanded. Greece may see weakness in her wan face and perceive her as the enchantress, but the reader begins to wonder if Helen, like Greece itself, is wan because she suffers from great weariness and sadness in the memory of "past ills."

In the final and longest stanza, reference is made to Helen being the daughter of Zeus, and love is mentioned for the first time. It is ironic that the love of which she was born was the seduction of her mother, Leda, by Zeus in the form of a swan. And the irony is intensified by Helen's seduction and abduction by Paris, a guest in her home. The final irony is that her country can only love her if she is laid in death's cold embrace. Having described her eyes, her smile, her hands, her slender knees, and her cool feet, the final image in the white motif is a Helen whose physical beauty has burned out until nothing is left but ash.

And ash, of course, is more than a white powder left from burning or the gray color of pallor suggestive of physical death. It is a genus of tree belonging to the olive family. The final words of the poem repeat the connection once more. The cypress too is a member of the olive family, its branches a symbol of mourning, as well as a gauzelike silk, worn for mourning when it has been dyed black.

—Donna Copeland, "Doolittle's 'Helen.'" *The Explicator* 46:4 (Summer 1988): p. 34.

DONNA KROLIK HOLLENBERG ON PATRIARCHY AND WOMAN'S PSYCHE

[Here Hollenberg examines this poem as representative of the damage inflicted on a woman's psyche through an oppressive patriarchy.]

In this chapter I consider the emotional matrix underlying the compressed surfaces of H.D.'s Imagist poetry. My view links questions of technique and sensibility, the laconic speech and "mythopoetic sense" noted by Ezra Pound, who invented the school of Imagism to describe H.D.'s poetry, with H.D.'s personal psychology. From her first book *Sea Garden* (1916) to *Red Roses for Bronze* (1931), H.D. provides startling insights into a woman poet's relation to her own creative power from the perspective of one whose sense of mastery in the experience of childbirth was seriously shaken. Some poems enact the miscarriage of psychic qualities associated with childbirth and the archetype of the child, such as hope and a sense of fulfillment. In others, she attempts to controvert these feelings of stricken imagination by divorcing female creative power from the ideologies of gender and the institutions of marriage and motherhood that circumscribe it. Some poems in this rebellious vein celebrate lesbian love as a refuge from the pain of heterosexual engagement. In many H.D. uses classical images of women to explore the discrepancy between her own experience and that already codified in culture. Because guilt partially blocked access to inner forms of her own, she projected her feelings, breathing new life into these figures of myth and classical poetry. Thus she conveyed the nonrational, overdetermined truths of dream in images from nature or Greek myth that were objective correlatives of her troubled emotional state. (. . .)

In its striking depiction of patriarchy's devastating impact on woman's psyche, H.D.'s "Helen" foreshadows her epic poem *Helen in Egypt*. The symbol of irresistible beauty and illicit love, the cause and goal of a terrible war, Helen has become an object of denigration and hatred: "All Greece reviles / the wan face when she smiles . . . remembering past enchantments / and past ills" (*CP*, 155). Overlooking her divine origin, the prophecy (made in Egypt in the *Odyssey*) that she is "God's daughter, born of love," Homeric epic has degraded her to a wan shadow of herself, sacrificing her to its heroic theme. The effect on her of this noxious cultural tradition, enacted in the poem, is increasing immobility and withdrawal. The once vital luster of her beauty turns to "white ash amid funereal cypresses" (*CP*, 155). As Susan Friedman has written, "Her smiles win her no mercy, and the only way she can become loved is through her death."

—Donna Krolik Hollenberg, "H.D.'s Imagism: A Poetry of Loss and Rebellion." *H.D.: The Poetics of Childbirth and Creativity* (Boston: Northeastern University Press, 1991): pp. 71, 90.

DIANA COLLECOTT ON HELEN'S EVOLUTION

[Here, Collecott traces H.D.'s characterization of Helen from an Imagist object to a Modernist subject in a search for faith and a new mode of woman's knowledge.]

In *Helen in Egypt,* the-heroine continues her questions:

> do you hear me? do I whisper?
> there is a voice within me,
> listen—let it speak for me. (175)

This feminine inner voice cannot be aligned with those ventriloquised by male authors: Henry James' Isabel Archer, Thomas Hardy's `woman much missed' (57) or James Joyce's Molly Bloom, for example. In his preface to *Portrait of a Lady* James asked: `By what process . . . is this slight "personality", the mere slim shade of an intelligent but presumptuous girl, to find itself endowed with the high attributes of a Subject?' (48). The much-discussed epic quest of

Helen in Egypt can also be construed as the process by which Helen, that 'slim shade', is recovered as subject from her object status in men's texts—from Homer's and Marlowe's silent icons, to the romantic fantasies of Poe and Yeats. Only in Euripides and Stesichorus, H.D.'s chosen sources, were those mute Helens identified as constructions of the masculine imagination. H.D. goes beyond her classical antecedents when she presents Helen as an object of exchange between men. Friedman has shown that the 1923 poem 'Helen' marks a critical moment in this process of recovery (*Psyche* 232–6), a starting point for what DuPlessis calls the 'major task of cultural recuperation in her deconstructed "epic"' (*Career* 108).

The recuperation of Helen as subject of her own story involves a narrative shift, which is also a shift in terms of gender and ideology; this is enunciated in the poet's introductory gloss on Stesichorus' palinode:

> *According to the Pallinode* [sic], *Helen was never in Troy. She had been transposed or translated from Greece into Egypt. Helen of Troy was a phantom, substituted for the real Helen, by jealous deities. The Greeks and the Trojans alike fought for an illusion.* (*Helen* I)

These textual metaphors, which recall the *substitution* of a 'phantom' for 'the real Helen', and her *translation* from Greece to Egypt, prepare the reader for her actual *transposition* in H.D.'s text from object to subject. 'She herself is the writing' (22) is the most emphatic and enigmatic statement in the prose accompanying the poem, added (as was James' preface to his *Portrait*) after its composition. For Claire Buck, this statement implies that Helen is presented to the reader 'as a script to be interpreted and translated' (155); we find in H.D.'s writing both a process of inscription and a Kristevan 'subject in process'. In the three lines of poetry quoted above, the containment of the subject pronoun *I* by the thrice-repeated object pronoun *me* spells out the meaning of the central line: 'there is a voice within me'. Pronominal wordplay is thus a significant feature of this late long poem, as it was in the punning prose of *Her*. Rachel DuPlessis has commented on the early novel: 'That object case used in the subject place [*her*/*Her*] exactly locates the thematics of the self-as-woman: "surveyor and sun-eyed", who pointedly explores the self-hood she can make from articulating her Otherness' (*Career* 61).

If this is true of the autobiographical subject Hermione, named for Helen's daughter, then it may also be true of the legendary figure Helen, for whom H.D.'s own mother was named. As we have seen, Helen of Troy entered H.D.'s poetry in *Heliodora* as the specular object and deleted subject of Homeric myth: the 'Helen' whom 'All Greece hates . . .' (*Collected* 154). She re-enters it, in all her other-ness, as the multiple personality explored in *Helen in Egypt*. That text effectively begins with our and Achilles' ignorance of who she is:

> . . . he
> knew not yet. Helen of Sparta.
> knew not Helen of Troy,
> knew not Helena, hated of Greece.   (14)

By analogy, the received history of modernism begins in ignorance of who H.D. is and what she wrote—including a damaging igno-rance of her longer, later, works. If, instead of being 'bound' by 'H.D., *Imagiste*', we follow the alternative strategy for reading H.D. proposed by Robert Duncan, taking *Helen in Egypt* as our starting point, we are struck by the work's handling of narrative, by its almost epic scale and by its use of speech. The voice of the poet, in the glosses that Pearson persuaded H.D. to write, counterpoints other voices: those of Theseus and Achilles, to be sure, but also 'an heroic voice, the voice of Helen of Sparta' (*Helen* 176). This voice speaks out from the confinement of the matter of Troy, confounding the assumption of some male critics that women writers have only one voice at their disposal—their own. Helen's expression 'let it speak for me' allows us to focus on utterance, on what is said, as well as on who is speaking

—Diana Collecott, "'the art of the future:' her emergence from Imagism." *H.D. and Sapphic Modernism, 1910–1950* (Cambridge: Cambridge University Press, 1999): pp. 146–148.

"The Walls Do Not Fall"

H.D. began writing "The Walls Do Not Fall" during World War II. She dedicated the forty-three stanza poem to her close friend, Bryher, and to Karnak, an ancient temple in Egypt, a country which H.D. believed to be sacred. She also noted her location in writing: London 1942. Here the title and her insistent notation of the place intersect. Like the walls of Troy which did not fall under a ten-year siege, the walls, perhaps most sensible in metaphoric terms, of language and of London did not fall under the constant bombardment of the Nazi Blitz. Instead, like the open temples at Karnak, they became sights of the sacred. H.D. chose to remain in London during the Blitz, believing that this exposure to war and to the valiant efforts of the British to carry on in the midst of mass destruction would not only make her a better artist, but it would help conquer her fear of war, created when she lost her brother in World War I. Ultimately, the experience created for the author a strange chrysalis period, during which time she developed a new sense of her relation to self and to the sacred.

She begins the poem with concrete images of a war-torn London. Rails are missing, having been melted down for munitions; churches and secular houses alike have been reduced to rubble, and London wears a gray pallor. Still, as the poet walks through the rumble "thoughts stir, inspiration stalks us/ through gloom." Even in the midst of destruction, the poet, (the narrator is most certainly the poet, that is her central relation to the subject), feels a strong desire to write, an impulse which answers the poem's primary thesis question posited at the end of the first stanza: "we passed the flame: we wonder/ what saved us? what for?" This quest to understand the machinations of divinity and to discover a suitable divinity, guides the rest of the poem. As in many of H.D.'s poems, gender plays a part in ascertaining a viable answer to both searches.

In the second stanza, she chronicles the debasement of the sacred, perhaps referring to Nazi propaganda as well as the institutionalization of religion. Still, she ultimately asks "how can you scratch out// indelible ink of the palimpsest/ of past misadventure?" This idea of the gods, the events of history, etc, being superimposed over each other, none ever completely forgotten, is a favorite of H.D.'s. Indeed, it is almost a statement of poetics. In the third stanza, H.D. manifests this notion when the rod of Aaron becomes also the rod of Caduseus, both representative of sacred power, though not of the same mythology. For the poet, this sacred sense exists in all things, the spiritual democracy crosses religious boundaries. To illustrate this, H.D. offers images ranging from mollusks to worms, each taking a period to develop the self and to embrace the sacred without outside influence. Over time, this breeds the artist and the scribe-prophet, a group of people integral to the survival of the world, much more so than the warrior, because these prophets carry the sacred Word.

In the seventh stanza, H.D. responds to the public notion that in times of war, art becomes inconsequential; she argues "but if you do not even understand what words say// how can you expect to pass judgement/ on what words conceal?" She contends words offer truth but they also conceal the idols of the past. In H.D.'s hands, words, like the women of Greek myth, possess depths and functions heretofore unconsidered by the patriarchy. The scribe is protected, "second only to the Pharaoh." because the Word will last; it is a form of immortality. She reminds readers that the sword is "the younger brother." The Judeo-Christian dogma states "in the beginning/ was the Word" thus supporting her contention that the Word and those who spread it are sacred beings, regardless of religion.

She interrupts her defense of the prophet-scribe and the Word with a vision of a god who is simultaneously Ra, Osiris and *Amen*, a version of the Christian God. Ultimately, the narrator comes to believe that the god is the Holy Ghost and the Holy Ghost is the Dream, a sort of laissez-faire between the sacred world and reality. Dreams explain the symbols still lurking in the palimpsest of history and the mind, and it then interprets them in today's language, making it comprehensible to the modern mind. Modernity also becomes important in reading the poem as the poem finds its purpose in creating new ways to uncover, understand and revise conventions of both language and myth.

In the twenty-first stanza, H.D. begins to play with language in earnest, showing that it is the mere semantics of words, rather than an essential truth, that appears to change the identity of gods: "here am I, Amen-Ra,/ Amen, Aries, the Ram;// time, time for you to begin a new spiral,/" Each incarnation urges the same spiritual quest and resurrection. So, when the poet is to be reborn from chrysalis to Psyche, the butterfly, she might just as easily become the Lady in "Tribute to the Angels" or Mary in "The Flowering of the Rod," which she does later in *Trilogy*. The holy being transcends the exclusivity of the institutions of language and religion. Still, in order to do that, to have that clarity of vision, the poet-scribe must release the rational, the "reasonable" and attend to something more primordial, older than language and that is experience and vision. This idea becomes slightly troubling because it excludes women's knowledge from that which is rational, although ultimately she suggests that women's knowledge of experience and vision are more valuable.

Language can serve to translate that spiritual experience but to do that, language too must be able to release its past:

> imagery
>
> done to death; perilous ascent,
> ridiculous descent; rhyme, jingle,
>
> overworked assonance, nonsense,
> juxtaposition of words for words' sake,
>
> without meaning, undefined; imposition,

The poet desires not only a rebirth and re-vision of the sacred but also a language that does not defile or trivialize it. Instead of creating verses for sentimental reasons, she suggests that artists "re-dedicate our gifts/ to spiritual realism." Art serves to validate an essential truth. In the final stanzas, H.D. asserts:

> there was One
>
> in the beginning, Creator, Fosterer, Begetter, the Same-forever
>
> in the papyrus-swamp
> in the Judean meadow."

Throughout the poem, H.D. gives the power of the sacred to all people, asserting that it is an innate quality developed during a chrysalis period. Then she claims that all gods are one, as if religion has been written on the same parchment over time, never fully erased, so that each god is never truly new, but simply a semantical and often syntactical mask superimposed over the god that came before. In this time of war, amidst destruction, the necessity for the strength of a single sacred notion becomes paramount. This poem acts as a cry for peace through faith and acknowledgement not of what has been destroyed but of what remains amidst the ruins: faith.

The poem ends in italics, suggesting a return to reality rather than the translation of the sub-conscious that the previous stanzas appear to be. In the midst of the bombing, she still does not know why the walls do not fall. Through the wreckage, the poet lives and continues to quest with the other initiates into language. This war brought with it the possibility for re-birth. She claims "we know no rule/ of procedure," and perhaps it is to their advantage. A new world order might be made, wherein the sacred is given precedence and the pen holds more power than the sword. In this way, "possibly we will reach haven,/ heaven."

"The Walls Do Not Fall"

SUSAN GUBAR ON LEXICAL REDISCOVERY

[In this extract, Gubar traces H.D.'s quest to rediscover the hidden meanings and sacred sense of words which still echo their prior incarnations.]

Modern words, too, may reveal hidden meanings, thereby relinquishing their alien impenetrability, if the poet can somehow perceive their coded, palimpsestic status. Fairly early in the *Trilogy*, H.D. manages to take some small comfort in the bitter joke wrapped in the pun "*cartouche*": for her contemporaries, it might mean a gun cartridge with a paper case, but she knows that it once signified the oblong figure in an Egyptian monument enclosing a sovereign's name (*WDNF,* 9). This kind of irony offers potential consolation when the poet realizes that it might still be possible to disentangle ancient meanings from corrupt forms, for instance the "Christos-image . . . from its art-craft junk-shop / paint-and-plaster medieval jumble // of pain-worship and death-symbol" (*WDNF*, 18). Finally the poet knows and feels

> the meaning that words hide;
>
> they are anagrams, cryptograms,
> little boxes, conditioned
>
> *to hatch butterflies* . . . [italics mine] (*WDNF*, 39)

H.D. learns how to decipher what that other H.D.—Humpty Dumpty—called "portmanteaus," words which open up like a bag or a book into compartments. By means of lexical reconstruction, she begins to see the possibility of purging language of its destructive associations and arbitrariness. Viewing each word as a puzzle ready to be solved and thereby freed not only of modernity but also of contingency, H.D. begins to hope that she can discover secret, coded messages. Surely these must be subversive to warrant their being so cunningly concealed by her culture.

Now The Walls Do Not Fall can end in a hymn to Osiris because the poet has managed to "recover the secret of Isis" (*WDNF*, 40). Just as H.D. is sure that the destructive signs surrounding her can be redefined for her own renewal, in the ancient myth Isis gathers together the scattered fragments of her lost brother/husband's body and reconstructs him in a happier ending than that to be enacted by the King's men for Humpty Dumpty. The resurrection of Osiris and the reconstruction of the magical power of the Word testify to the healing, even vivifying powers of the poet-Isis who can now see the unity between Osiris and Sirius. Since Sirius is the star representing Isis come to wake her brother from death, such an equation means that the poet glimpses the shared identity of the sibling lovers Osiris and Isis. Approaching this "serious" mystery, H.D. asks, "O, Sire, is" this union between the god and the goddess finally possible (*WDNF*, 42)? She can even connect "Osiris" with the "zrr-hiss" of war-lightning. The poet who uses words with reverence can release the coded messages contained or enfolded within them. She has found the "alchemist's key" which "unlocks secret doors" (*WDNF*, 30). Although the walls still do not fall, continuing to testify to the divisions and barriers between people, between historical periods, within consciousness itself, they also preserve remnants of written messages—anagrams and cryptograms—which, by providing the link from the present back to the past, allow H.D. to evade the destructive definitions of reality provided by those who utilize the word for modern mastery.

—Susan Gubar, "The Echoing Spell of H.D.'s *Trilogy.*" *Contemporary Literature* 19:2 (Spring 1978): pp. 206–207.

Susan Stanford Friedman on H.D.'s Use of the Syncretist Tradition

[Susan Stanford Friedman is the Virginia Woolf Professor of English and Women's Studies at the University of Wisconsin-Madison. She is the author of *Mappings: Feminism and the Cultural Geographies of Encounter* as well as two books on H.D. Here, she examines H.D.'s use of the syncretist tradition as a tool for understanding sacred signs in times of extremity.]

H.D.'s esoteric research into the syncretist traditions of "la Sagesse" becomes the foundation of poetic identity in the world of the poem. Robert Ambelain, Jean Chaboseau, Denis de Rougemont, and W. B. Crow had all described for H.D. a protean tradition of mysticism and hermetic wisdom "born of one mother"—that is, originating in a common source. In the *Trilogy*, the poet announces her initiation into that religious tradition and explores her artistic contribution to the secret "mystery," whose forms are ever changing, whose essence is ever the same. As mythmaker, H.D. did not see herself as an isolated creator of new mythologies. She instead experienced a spiritual bond with a community of initiates who are "companions in this mystery," "companions of the flame." Echoing H.D.'s own alienation from any religious organizations, orthodox or heterodox, the poet's snarled greetings and speechless communication with her companions suggest that H.D. was not referring to formal initiation into a group like the Theosophical Society or the Order of 15. Rather, initiation develops out of the poet's knowledge of "secret symbols" and her sense of belonging to an ongoing, hidden tradition kept alive by others like her.

H.D.'s announcement of identification with esoteric tradition in section thirteen is itself a text whose images simultaneously reveal and conceal hermetic dimensions of meaning. Decoded with the help of other sections in the poem and H.D.'s esoteric sources, this section strongly links the *Trilogy* to the syncretist tradition described by Ambelain and others. H.D. used the concepts of the Gnostics and the Ophites, for example, to build her metaphors of Psyche's search for rebirth in a death-centered world at war. The Gnostics in particular developed the doctrine of the soul's preexistence in the realm of the spirit. At the birth of a child, an unwilling soul is assigned to the imperfect world of manifest form to live out its life cycle, trapped in the human body. For the soul forever yearning to return "home," death is a liberation from the bonds of the flesh, an experience that purifies the soul from the taint of material existence. Material death is simultaneously spiritual birth, or more accurately rebirth. Within this context, the Gnostics regarded Jehovah, the god of Genesis and the creator of material forms, as a temperamental lesser deity who jealously guarded the Tree of Knowledge so that the souls attached to Adam and Eve could not rejoin the spiritual realm of pure wisdom.

The Ophites, a mystical sect that flourished in the century before Jesus' birth, developed related doctrines of resurrection as they decoded the esoteric meanings in Genesis. The Ophites worshipped the serpent of Genesis as a symbol of rebirth and condemned Jehovah for cursing the serpent in the Garden of Eden and consigning the human race to ignorance and death. The serpent, long associated with resurrection in many Near Eastern religions, offered Eve knowledge of the Divine One and the eternal life of the spirit. Like Prometheus and Asklepios in the Greek tradition, the serpent was punished for its attempted gift to the human race. The Ophite attempt to transcend the spiritual limitations imposed by Jehovah revolved around worship of the serpent and all others who had rebelled against tyranny, including such conventionally maligned figures as Lucifer and Lilith. H.D. read about Ophite doctrine in Ambelain's *Adam, dieu rouge*: "In the beginning of Genesis or *Sepher Bereschit*, the serpent, we know, symbolizes the Supreme Being, Elohim, the adversary of the Creator of the Material World. The serpent awakened the intelligence of Man and Woman by making them eat the fruit of the Tree of Knowledge. This is why the serpent became the symbol of Medicine and the symbol of the Saviour."

H.D.'s image of the "old self" as "shroud" enclosing the newly emerging self identified with other companions in mystery develops Gnostic and Ophite doctrines to portray the central action and symbolism of *The Walls Do Not Fall*. Adapting the syncretist process of esoteric tradition, H.D. fused the Ophite serpent and Gnostic soul to create the poem's recurring image of the human spirit struggling to survive and transcend the Nazi engines of death. The "shroud" is a reference to the poet's frequent portrayal of herself as a "worm"-elsewhere in the poem:

> In me (the worm) clearly
> is no righteousness, but this—
>
> persistence; I escaped spider-snare,
> bird-claw, scavenger bird-beak,
>
> clung to grass-blade,
> the back of a leaf

when storm-wind
tore it from its stem;

I escaped, I explored
rose-thorn forest,

was rain-swept
down the valley of a leaf;

. . . .

. . . I profit
by every calamity;

I eat my way out of it;
gorged on vine-leaf and mulberry,

parasite, I find nourishment:
when you cry in disgust,

a worm on the leaf,
a worm in the dust,

a worm on the ear-of-wheat,
I am yet unrepentant,

for I know how the Lord God
is about to manifest, when I,

the industrious worm,
spin my own shroud.   (*T.*, 11–12)

The diminution of the human is faintly mock-heroic, the craft is strikingly imagist, but the symbolic associations of the poet's self-portrait are distinctly esoteric. The "industrious worm" who spins her own shroud is H.D.'s version of the Gnostic soul whose human "garment" is a shroud of material existence and morality. The defiant persistence of the "worm's" journey through a storm-tossed, mocking world is analogous to the Gnostic's belief that the soul is out of place in its material form and yearns to complete its life cycle to be free. The poet echoes Gnostic language in her reference to her companions who have "done their worm-cycle" and to the "latter-day twice-born . . . dragging the forlorn husk of self" (*T.*, 15, 22). The soul's second birth leaves behind the "old self" and initiates the new self into the service of "this mystery," the Sophia of Gnostic tradition.

While developing Gnostic notions of rebirth, H.D. nonetheless shifted the grounds of spiritual alienation considerably. The Gnostic soul's disgust for the flesh in general and sexuality in particular has little relevance to the *Trilogy*. The world of material existence that the soul yearns to transcend becomes in H.D.'s poem the modern world at war and the materialist perspective that would deny spiritual realism. Initiation or rebirth in H.D.'s symbolic system is not the Gnostic escape from the world of forms, but the soul's discovery of the esoteric wisdom underlying the hieroglyphs of war. The persistent "worm" spins its cocoon and becomes a butterfly, one of the "companions of the flame":

> we pull at this dead shell,
> struggle but we must wait
>
> till the new Sun dries off
> the old-body humours; (*T.*, 22)

In the "*condensare*" of syncretism, however, the "worm" as caterpillar is simultaneously the Ophite serpent. "*Be ye wise* / as asps, scorpions, as *serpents*," the poet warns, and her "worm" persona links her with esoteric symbols of resurrection and wisdom. The "you" of orthodox traditions have made the "worm" a symbol of death, by metonymy the agent of corporeal disintegration. A "worm on a leaf / a worm in the dust" inspires disgust and represents the mortal, not divine, aspect of human nature. But the "we" of esoteric traditions recognize the lowly worm as the serpent cursed by Jehovah. This serpent, the poet learns in the process of spiritual transformation, is the same as the healing serpents entwined on the winged Caduceus of Hermes Psychopompous; the uraeus worn by Egyptian deities and pharaohs; the horned headdress of Hathor, associated by H.D. with insect antennae; and the serpent rod of the biblical magician Aaron. The shortest section in *The Walls Do Not Fall* condenses serpent and insect into the single image of the worm, and it synthesizes Greek, Egyptian, and Hebrew traditions into a single current of esoteric wisdom:

> Gods, goddesses
> wear the winged head-dress
>
> of horns, as the butterfly
> antennae,
>
> or the erect king-cobra crest
> to show how the worm turns. (*T.*, 13)

Conventional associations triggered by "the worm turns" suggest the inevitable processes of decay after burial in the earth as the worm "turns" in the dead flesh it consumes. But esoteric translation of this death symbol transforms the movement of "turning" into the processes of metamorphosis. The lowly "worm in the dust" industriously spins the cocoon of its own rebirth. Similarly, the poet-initiate "turns" the evil serpent of Genesis into the redemptive symbol of wisdom through her association with esoteric tradition. Along with her "companions in this mystery," she can use the "secret symbols" she has learned to discover hidden dimensions of meaning in conventional religions.

Even more importantly, however, her association with mystical traditions allows her to decode the runes of material reality, the rubble of war. She and her fellow initiates are "companions of the flame" as well as "companions in this mystery." To interpret the "flame" of war, she and her companions abandon the conventional ethics of the Judeo-Christian tradition. She calls herself a worm without "righteousness"; she is "indifferent to your good and evil." Like the Gnostics, Ophites, and Luciferians before her, the poet discards the orthodox definitions of evil and proceeds to find the symbols of Sagesse in the heart of death itself. The "flames" of death become the purifying fire of rebirth. By extension the fiery destruction of London becomes the apocalypse that will usher in the new age of Aquarius, a "woman's age" as H.D. wrote to Viola Jordan (2 July 1941). The meaning of the word "apocalypse" itself fuses the hermetic significance of fire and the process of revelation. As William Loftus Hare wrote in a book H.D. read carefully, an "apocalypse" is not only a redemptive cataclysm, but also "the *revelation* or *uncovering* of something by the expedient of obtaining a point of view from which it can be seen in its true significance (*apo*— removal from a place; *kalupto*—to envelop, to conceal, to darken)." The task of the poet-prophet is the "uncovering" of spiritual realism enveloped in the dark flame of war.

—Susan Stanford Friedman, "'Companions of the Flame'." *Psyche Reborn: The Emergence of H.D.* (Bloomington: Indiana University Press, 1981): pp. 214–219.

[Here, Friedman views H.D.s quest to transcend the reality
of war to discover the sacred as representative of some characteristic Modernist elements in "The Walls Do Not Fall."]

The Walls Do Not Fall, the first poem in the *Trilogy*, records the
poet's attempt to translate the hidden meaning of external reality.
Like much modernist literature, however, this quest is permeated
with despair engendered by the "real" world whose message is at
best ambivalent. *The Walls* ends with a starkly rendered expression
of the modernist nightmare world:

> *Still the walls do not fall,*
> *I do not know why;*
>
> *there is zrr-hiss,*
> *lightning is a not-known,*
>
> *unregistered dimension;*
> *we are powerless,*
>
> *dust and powder fill our lungs*
> *our bodies blunder*
>
> *through doors twisted on hinges,*
> *and the lintels slant*
>
> *cross-wise;*
> *we walk continually*
>
> *on thin air*
> *that thickens to a blind fog,*
>
> *then step swiftly aside,*
> *for even the air*
>
> *is independable,*
> *thick where it should be fine*
>
> *and tenuous*
> *where wings separate and open,*
>
> *and the ether*
> *is heavier than the floor,*

and the floor sags
like a ship floundering;

we know no rule
of procedure,

we are voyagers,
discoverers of the not-known,

the unrecorded;
we have no map;

possibly we will reach haven,
heaven.   *(T., 58–59)*

The techniques of imagism are used to describe concretely the physical reality to suggest the correlative and collective state of mind of
the modern world. The dust, powder, and smoke from the bombs
suffocate and blind the spirit of the ruined city; bodies lurch in the
rubble without security and direction. Doorways lead to nowhere,
and the city is a "floundering ship." Cultural symbols and traditions
can offer no direction any more. Simple facts are clear, but their significance—if they have any—is hidden in the spiritual fog. The "zrr-
hiss" and lightning flashes in the sky are certainly bombs, but they
may contain a sign from some "unregistered dimension," some alternate reality. The "wings that separate and open" release destruction,
but suggest also the protective wings of angels. "We are powerless"
in the face of reality, but not ultimately paralyzed. With full knowledge of material reality, the poet will take an existential leap of faith
to begin the search for transcendent reality—we are voyagers, discoverers of the not-known / the unrecorded." What gives this quest
its particular modernist quality is the recognition of potential failure
and the underlying uncertainty of goal. Who runs the castle in
Kafka's *Castle*; is there even a castle that sends messages? Who is
Godot in Beckett's *Waiting for Godot*; if he even exists, is he benev-
olent? Without any tangible evidence to validate the search, the poet
must act as if there were an alternate life-giving reality to be discovered or created, "possibly we will reach haven, / heaven." We
may or may not reach an end-point in this quest; the safe "haven"
from death may or may not be "heaven." Living in a world that
defines reality empirically, the poet must nonetheless continue the
search for the "unregistered dimension" that can incorporate as it
transcends that reality.

—Susan Stanford Friedman, "'Companions of the Flame'." *Psyche Reborn: The Emergence of H.D.* (Bloomington: Indiana University Press, 1981): pp. 104–105.

CAROLYN FORCHÉ ON H.D. AS A PRECURSOR

[Carolyn Forché teaches in the MFA Program in Poetry at George Mason University. She is the author of several books of poetry and criticism, including *The Angel of History* for which she received the Los Angeles Times Book Award. Here, she considers H.D. as a literary antecedent, struggling to create a language of resurrection that also acknowledged the devastation that preceded it.]

"The Walls Do Not Fall" is an assertion of a poet's will. Of course the walls fell, trembling and temporal, stone by stone as once they had been erected. It was language that went on, the language that, according to Pound, "civilized Greece and Rome" (1960: 33), the language, according to poet Paul Celan, that was not lost in spite of all that happened. "But it had to go through its own lack of answers, through terrifying silence, through the thousand darknesses of murderous speech" (Celan 1986: 34)

The intricacies of poetic influence and linkage can be amorphous, tenuous, and indirect, unreadable and indiscernible but for the assertions of the practitioner, who recognizes the effects of a forerunner upon her art. I prefer this to the "strong" influence of misprision postulated by Harold Bloom, while acknowledging this formulation among possible others. My first H.D. schooled my early poetic thought, but it was decades before I would discover the confluence of circumstance, affinity, and shared knowledge that would characterize my apprehension of her later work. My second book, *The Country between Us*, marked a departure from the first in retaining a poetic subjectivity confident of the legitimacy of subjective reportage but as yet unaware of the reconfigurative power of the experience of extremity. It seemed sufficient that the "I" interrogate and question itself within the accepted lyric-narrative form, calling into question its assertions and pronouncements. That such work could be dismissed as the product of a certain political intentionality was disturbing, but I had not yet begun to apprehend the meaning of self, time, and language in the aftermath of mass death.

Five years after the publication of my second book I wrote the first draft of *The Angel of History*. Several months later I encountered my second H.D., the poet of *Trilogy*, while gathering work for *Against Forgetting: Twentieth-Century Poetry of Witness*, a compilation of the works of 145 poets, writing in over 30 languages, who had themselves endured conditions of extremity during the twentieth century. The project was one of opening a space for the reading of such works, as the evidential art of endurance in the context of unimaginable horror.

The whole of Western thought seemed heretofore conditioned on a concept of the self as a rational monad: Hegel had demonstrated the rational in concrete history, and Heidegger had shown that the root of history lies in the historicity of the human being, grounding a deeper understanding of the meaning of human existence in the particulars of concrete experience. Poetry of my time had, it seemed, built a *cordon sanitaire* around particular historical circumstance, isolating it from philosophic and artistic query (see Wyschogrod 1985). It seemed that the subjective "I," however challenged and interrogated, could not survive the collapse of representation, and so I endeavored to create a text that would subsume subjectivity, relegating it to the role of passive recorder: the angel Metatron who listened but could not intervene, like the *deus abscondi* of the Holocaust. Absent this God, perhaps divine interlocutors could be supposed. Perhaps it was possible to move beyond the paradigm of authenticity and the primacy of the interpersonal sphere. The dissolution of this "I" opened the possibility of an I–Thou consciousness (after Martin Buber), spiritually dialectical and awake, vibrant and reciprocal, that would somehow enable the consideration of responsibility, of our ability to respond.

If personal death had been hitherto the touchstone of moral stature, marking the worth of an individual's life, what would mass-death become but the shifting tectonic plate of our sense of collective being? We mark the passing of extinct life forms while we ourselves are in the process of vanishing forever. The assurance of future time recedes from certainty. Life and death become copresent.

Our consciousness of time is no longer sequential and synchronous but spatial and diachronic, H.D.'s living present. We are in the realm of the "death event," wherein "event designates the nexus of dynamic but ephemeral occurrences, the 'pieces of flotsam combed from the historical ocean,' that, taken together, form the segments of a single meaning constellation. This pattern becomes generative for the self-understanding of its time (even if this understanding is only partially glimpsed by contemporaries)" (Braudel 1972: 1243).

What I recognized in *Trilogy* was the affirmation of a precursor struggling with the insurmountable difficulty of writing her way toward restoration while conceiving a poetic form that would somehow display the ruin. However, unlike H.D., I wanted to retain hope while jettisoning the possibility of redemption (a possibility denied by spiritual refusal in the steps of Simone Weil). *The Angel of History* would be a noneschatological, nonredemptive work, denying itself the salvific comforts of a preruptural voice, speaking as though the historical cataclysm had not occurred. Yet I see in it traces of H.D., for if a consciousness suffuses H.D.'s *Trilogy*, in its transforming, recuperative rewriting of Judeo-Christian thought, it is the consciousness, however oblique and unrealized, of the extermination of the Jews and its prescience of the dawning of the nuclear age.

So in recognizing this second H.D., I recognize an influence ipso facto, an affinity with the work of a precursor who struggled toward the cataclysm that was to constitute a black hole in the cosmos of Western thought. We cannot live, as Edmund Husserl has written, if "to live is always to live-in-certainty of the world, being constantly and directly 'conscious' of the world and of oneself as living in the world" (1970: 142–43). But it is possible to live provisionally beyond the rupture and to write our way out of the ruin, aware of the fragility of civilization and the impossibility—indeed undesirability—of achieving "closure," if this means cordoning off the past as if we could escape it. It is her courage before this difficulty that most astounds me.

—Carolyn Forché, "H.D. After H.D." *H.D. and Poets After*. (Iowa City: University of Iowa Press, 2000): pp. 262–265.

[Georgina Taylor is an English teacher at St. Bartholomew's
School in Newbury. Here, she discusses H.D.'s poem as a
response to and a part of a public healing process.]

There are many different ways in which texts of the period, in fact,
very deliberately participated in a healing process. The 1940s are of
course most often associated with the neo-religious writing of Auden
and, most famously, Eliot's *Four Quartets*. The work of Edith
Sitwell of this period came closest to this, using conventional
Christian symbolism to write of resurrection and regeneration, part
of the wave of writers turning to religious symbolism and Romantic
forms in their writing, including Kathleen Raine, David Gascoyne,
George Barker, and Dylan Thomas. H.D. too drew on Christian symbolism, however, her work is far more eclectic than that of Sitwell,
Raine, Eliot, or Auden. Her *Trilogy* fused conventional Christian
symbolism with mysticism, astrology, and hermeticism—different
belief systems were brought together in a quest towards healing.
Trilogy both presents the problem and, as *The Gift* does, works to
heal. The first section, *The Walls Do Not Fall*, is H.D.'s most sophis-
ticated and thorough exploration of the anger and aggression inside
all people; there is no 'they' who are violent as against an 'us' who
are not:

> We have seen how the most amiable,
> under physical stress,
>
> become wolves, jackals,
> mongrel curs;
>
> We know further that hunger
> may make hyenas of the best of us;

One of the speakers desires to be eaten by the god *Amen*, to allow a
masochistic fantasy to be acted out as a religious rite." The lowest
and the highest of humanity's desires become inextricably fused;
there must be a painstaking examination of motive and symbolism
in order to begin to separate these out. Meanwhile, the subconscious
landscape is one of fish devouring fish, and of threat from octopus
or shark and other 'incongruent monsters'. By understanding per-

sonal aggression, the aggression of the 'enemy' becomes better understood, and *Trilogy* allows for development and progress towards healing rather than simply charting the problem. Out of suffering new understanding can emerge; the worm 'profit[s] / by every calamity' and is able to draw life and creativity—however fevered and momentary—out of destruction, in a process akin to Eliot's redeeming and purifying fire:

> in the rain of incendiary,
> other values were revealed to us,
>
> other standards hallowed us;
> strange texture, a wing covered us,
>
> and though there was a whirr and roar in the high air,
> there was a Voice louder,
>
> though its speech was lower
> than a whisper.

—Georgina Taylor, "Responses to the World in Crisis." *H.D. and the Public Sphere of Modernist Women Writers, 1913–1946* (Oxford: Clarendon Press, 2001): pp. 172–173.

"Tribute to the Angels"

H.D. begins this second poem of *Trilogy* with the last line of "The Walls Do Not Fall:" ". . .possibly we will reach haven, heaven." In this new incarnation, the meaning of the line changes with the introduction of Hermes Trismegistus, thought by writers of the first and second centuries to be tracts written by the Egyptian god, Thoth. These writings introduced the Philosopher's stone said to possess the power to turn base metals into gold, to be the secret of life and health, to be spiritually significant and to represent pure thought and selflessness. A fundamental axiom guides these texts: *As above, so below.* This posits the world as a reflection of heaven and the divine, both home to the sacred. That being the case, the last line of "The Walls Do Not Fall" becomes a quest to make earth as heaven, a doctrine espoused by a host of religions. This idea shapes the first stanza and guides the rest of the poem, which, like the poems surrounding it, consists of 43 stanzas almost exclusively in coupled lines. She invokes Hermes Trismegistus and Mithra as examples, urging poets and orators to rediscover the wisdom lost over time, the wisdom that might create a heaven on earth.

> re-invoke, re-create
> opal, onyx, obsidian,
>
> now scattered in the shards
> men tread upon.

These lines also accuse men, the patriarchy, of destroying and then treading over the remains of all that they have destroyed, whether that be the rights of women or the sacred texts and gods of a past faith. In large part, H.D.'s quest is to recompose faith from the remains of old religions, particularly those that believed in women as beings equally sacred to men.

In the second stanza, a prophetic voice tells the poet that "Your walls do not fall, he said,/ because your walls are made of jasper;" a sacred stone found in the Bible, most notably in the breast plate of the high priest amidst eleven other stones. When the poet sees this vision of jasper, the stone she envisions does not fit the shape of the breastplate; rather, it suggests the necessity of change, of finding a new priest/priestess to take possession of the stone. In the third stanza, H.D. invokes John the Apostle, who brought prophecy of the Apocalypse in seven seals. H.D. contextualizes him for the reader. He saw the seven stars in the hands of Christ representing the seven fold power of God, the seven churches, figured as seven women that took hold of one man (Christ) and seventy-times-seven, the times one must forgive the transgressions of others. He introduces, somewhat paradoxically, both notions of forgiveness and of the Apocalypse wherein all shall be judged.

The impending doom prophesized by John seems real to H.D. who lived through the apocalyptic Blitz when the fiery breath of God could easily be equated with the dropping of bombs. She recognized in her poem that she lived in a time when peace would not be known, that the seven angels of the Apocalypse would come down and destroy the world she knew. Indeed, her voice echoes the prophetic tone of the Apostle. In the seventh stanza, H.D. gives praise to the most destructive angel among the seven, Uriel. In praising him, she acknowledges that only through death could there be rebirth. For H.D., the idea of a metaphorical death of the self is very important in the evolution of the artist and the woman; it becomes, in a way, a part of the chrysalis stage that so obsessed her in "The Walls Do Not Fall."

In the eighth stanza, she complicates the notion of death again; this time, it is the death of meaning. From the word Mary, she takes the dual meanings bitter and mother and melts them down into one idea, a fusion of all the meaning that has come before, and from this, she creates a jewel, a kind of philosopher's stone, possessed of sacred qualities.

She begins to question the nature of this dual jewel, that is both bitter and fiercely maternal. She questions as mother, as poet, as a practitioner of roles both masculine and feminine. Her search leads her to reconsider the incarnations of the mother in myth, from Mary to Venus and the ways in which words betray the origins of the gods, changing Venus from veneration to venery. This poem works closely with its predecessor in deconstructing the political agenda of language as an active attempt to desecrate non-Christian gods and women.

The jewel elicits both color and fragrance which the poet tries to quantify and when she cannot, she is told to invent it, positing the poet as an Adamic figure, capable of naming all that she discovers. However, the poet differs here from Adam, from the patriarchal inclination to own through language, instead, she wants to experience it directly in all its multiplicity, an experience which she wants to share with her audience as she indicated through her use of the inclusive first person plural and the direct address of second person. H.D. illustrates through the seven angels, one of death, one of life, one of peace, one of war, that each needs the other to live and to sustain its own strength. Without war, peace cannot be truly understood and so on. This multiplicity, seen everywhere, eliminates the need for churches and temples. For those with the desire and the power to see, the world becomes a sacred place. H.D. sees the manifestation of this idea when she passes a half-burned tree, still flowering. Again, the palimpsestic quality of H.D.'s poetry and circle of allusions adds to the depth of the image. The flowering tree recalls its brother in the rod of Aaron, which flowered to indicate God's sanctioning of Aaron's authority. The rod is also traditionally associated with male power. By giving it procreative powers, she suggests that the source of spiritual power is androgynous or possibly entirely female. H.D. reads the flowering of the tree as a sign from God that life will continue, female power will be recovered and the sacred shall be revealed.

The revelation comes in a dream for the poet. In it, H.D. is sitting with friends when the Lady knocks and comes into the room. Before she can ask her any questions, H.D. awakes, aware for the first time that the Lady was a dream. "The Walls Do Not Fall" becomes important in interpreting the dream because H.D. explains in that poem that dreams connect the sacred to reality. In trying to offer the vision to the reader, she lists in detail the different invocations of the Lady created by men throughout history; her vision differs from all. She sees the Lady as wearing white, sitting without child, without any of the attributes that make her important as a vessel in the Church. Here the motherhood is spiritual rather than actual as in the case of Christ. H.D. lists bitterly how the patriarchy prides itself on its treatment of Mary; they "have done very well by her." They made her pretty and tall, veiled and silenced. In H.D.'s vision however, she becomes more than that limited icon. Her white gown represents inclusion, of all colors and all the faiths that have come before. Similarly, H.D. chronicles the shift from the rod of Caduseus to the rod of Aaron, from Thoth to Hermes to the archangels, indicating that all have sprung from the same source.

In the vision, the Lady appears pleased with the poet and her friends:

> who did not forgo our heritage
>
> at the grave-edge;
> she must have been pleased
>
> with the straggling company of the brush and quill
> who did not deny their birthright;

The Lady also carries with her a blank book, The Book of Life, according to the poet, and it is blank, ready to be written and re-visioned, and the Lady herself is being reborn from her incarnations as Mary, as Isis, as Venus. Her book then becomes:

> . . . our book; written
> or unwritten, its pages will reveal
>
> a tale of a Fisherman,
> a tale of a jar or jars,
>
> the same—different—the same attributes,
> different yet the same as before.

H.D. emphasizes yet again that the same sacred truth will be found regardless of the book in which it is written or the tongue in which it is spoken or the being that delivers it. This powerfully suggests that this time the sacred experience shall be writ by women.

The poem ends bringing the poet back into the war again, suggesting that this vision of a Mary melted down and re-born mirrors that of London and that of the artist. From this alchemist's stone, the sacred is born and the city risen. The flowering of the rod again signifies God's sanctioning, this time of the artist's and the city's rise from the dead.

"Tribute to the Angels"

ALBERT GELPI ON H.D.'S ARCHETYPE OF WOMAN

[Albert Gelpi is a Professor Emeritus at Stanford University. He is the author of *Emily Dickinson: The Mind of the Poet, The Tenth Muse: The Psyche of the American Poet, A Coherent Splendor: The American Poetic Renaissance 1910–1950* and *Living In Time: The Poetry of C. Day Lewis.* He was also the founding editor of *Cambridge Studies in American Literature and Culture* and editor of numerous books. Here he elucidates H.D.'s attempts in *Trilogy* to re-member the female archetype as a composite of historical and sacred women, both from mythology and the poet's past.]

Tribute to the Angels was written in a fortnight during "a wonderful pause just before D-Day" as "a sort of premature peace poem." (*T,* ix) The unexpected epiphany which generated this spring poem occurred on a London bus when H.D. glimpsed a charred apple-tree flowering again amidst the rubble of a burned out square. Hermes Trismegistus (Thoth) and St. John are still present at the beginning of the sequence. However, Hermes leads to Aphrodite; Christos, to Mary. Their animus-inspiration directs the poem through the divination of the angels to an astonishing manifestation of the feminine.

The angels of St. John's Revelation who attend the divine throne appear as emissaries, and four of the seven have been named and addressed—Raphael (Birth), Gabriel (Change), Azrael (Death), and Uriel (the fire of God's judgment and will)—before the first premonition of the archetypal feminine, whose appearance is rendered as alchemical "Transubstantiation" (87):

> Now polish the crucible
> and in the bowl distill
>
> a word most bitter, *marah,*
> a word bitterer still, *mar,*
>
> sea, brine, breaker, seducer,
> giver of life, giver of tears;

Now polish the crucible
and set the jet of flame

under, till *marah–mar*
are melted, fuse and join

and change and alter,
mer, mere, mere, mater, Maia, Mary,

Star of the Sea,
Mother. (71)

The bitter and destructive sea, nature's womb and tomb, becomes the virgin-mother" goddess. "Star of the Sea," an epithet from the Litany of the Blessed Virgin, precipitates the association of Mary with "Venus, Aphrodite, Astarte" who appears in double aspect as a star, "Phosphorus/at sun-rise,/Hesperus at sun-set" (73). This evocation of the feminine calls forth the fifth angel, Annael, the peace of God, designated by H.D. as the Mohammedan Venus, and linked in turn with the Hebrew Anna, Hannah or Grace (*T*, ix). Moreover, she appears in a syzygy with Uriel, the angel of God's fiery breath; the pair intimates the Sancta Spiritus: "So we hail them together,/one to contrast the other" (80). After this annunciation God's bride blooms in war-torn London: "We see her visible and actual,/beauty incarnate" in the miraculous spring-flowering of the scorched tree in a garden-square behind a demolished house (82–83).

Then all unexpected, the vision of the Lady, first in a dream in which she appeared to H.D. and two women friends. Remembering perhaps the triune goddesses in "Triplex," the poet wonders whether "we three together" could summon the supernatural; "yet it was all natural enough, we agreed" (90). For when the poet wakens from the dream the Presence is "there more than ever,/as if she had miraculously/related herself to time here" (91). Who is this Lady? Earlier in the poem, when

my patron [Freud or Bryher or both] said, "name it";

I said, I can not name it,
there is no name;

he said,
"invent it." (76)

So here, the patron's voice in her head tells her that if she cannot define the Lady by name she can at least invent images. Though the Lady be a Presence and "no rune nor riddle" (84), the scribe suggests her mysterious charisma in rich details from the Renaissance painters and their pre-Raphaelite imitators:

> Our Lady of the Goldfinch,
> Our Lady of the Candelabra,
>
> Our Lady of the Pomegranate,
> Our Lady of the Chair;
>
> we have seen her, an empress,
> magnificent in pomp and grace,
>
> and we have seen her
> with a single flower
>
> or a cluster of garden-pinks
> in a glass beside her;
>
> we have seen her snood
> drawn over her hair,
>
> or her face set in profile
> with the blue hood and stars;
>
> we have seen her head bowed down
> with the weight of a domed crown,
>
> or we have seen her, a wisp of a girl
> trapped in a golden halo. . . . (93)

H.D. goes on to designate the voice which delineates these images, gorgeous though are, as "you"—not her truest voice, but Bryher's or Freud's voice in her mind, turning her to aesthetic inventions for the Lady. Without taking back any of the gorgeous images, the voice of "I," H.D. speaking for herself, insists that the Lady, far from being "a hieratic figure, the veiled Goddess" (as "you would have her") is more human and approachable: a Vestal, perhaps, of the *Bona Dea*, but in any case a living reality, no mere art-image. In fact, as it turns out, "she is Psyche, the butterfly,/out of the cocoon" at last (103).

The Lady is, then, the apotheosis of the Self. Her specific character, as she manifested herself in H.D.'s bedside that night in 1944, is disclosed when she is paired with the sixth angel, Michael, earlier linked to Thoth and Hermes and here "regent of the planet Mercury" (99). H.D. suggested to Pearson that "she is the Troubador or Poet's Lady," (*T*, ix), but in fact she is something more than muse. She is H.D.'s archetype: the troubadour as woman, the woman as troubador, the woman-troubadour herself. In her arms the Lady bears no Son ("the Child was not with her," 97, "the Lamb was not with her," 104) but instead her writings: "she looked so kindly at us/under her drift of veils,/and she carried a book" (100). The Madonna anticipated earlier ("Star of the Sea/Mother") turns out to be the Virgin-Scribe. What's more, the book that is "our book" (105) is in fact H.D.'s poem in the reader's hand:

> She carried a book, either to imply
> she was one of us with us,
>
> or to suggest she was satisfied
> with our purpose, a tribute to the Angels. . . . (107)

Just as the revelation of the masculine as scribe and psychopomp in *The Walls Do Not Fall* opened the way to the revelation of the Virgin-Scribe in *Tribute to the Angels*, so the Virgin-Scribe makes possible a fuller exfoliation of the feminine archetype in *The Flowering of the Rod*, and preparation for that further exfoliation summons the masculine once more. The seventh and last angel is Zadkiel:

> regent of Jupiter,
> or Zeus-pater or Theus-pater,
>
> *Theus*, God; God-the-father, father-god
> or the Angel god-father,
>
> himself, heaven yet at home in a star. . . . (108)

Such is the scribe's witness: "I John saw. I testify" (109). The final address to Zadkiel specifically foreshadows the third poem in the image of the Lady's "face like a Christmas-rose" (110). So the spring poem of the angels and the Lady grows into a Christmas poem, *The Flowering of the Rod*, dated December 18–31, 1944. It is the book the Lady holds. Though the Lady's book is blank when she appears in *Tribute to the Angels*, it is announced as "a tale of a Fisherman/a tale of a jar or jars" (105), the third sequence of *Trilogy*.

The tale of the Fisherman and the two jars of Kaspar—the jar the Wise Man presented to Mary and the Christ-child at His birth and the twin-jar Mary Magdalene later used to anoint Him for His death—is both traditional and heterodox. Jesus and the two Marys; but the episodes are here told in inverted chronological order. The poem first presents the anointing by Magdalene, the reformed courtesan, and ends with the stable at Bethlehem, and the narrative order corresponds to H.D. deepening engagement with the mother archetype. The alienation from the mother with whom she felt deep religious and artistic affinity had thwarted her psychological realization of herself as woman and mother. She brooded over her miscarriage of Aldington's baby during the war; when she bore Cecil Gray's child in 1919, she called her Perdita, the lost one, and had difficulty in assuming and fulfilling the mothering role. On Corfu the year after Perdita's birth she took Athena Nike, the motherless maiden-daughter of Zeus, as "my own especial sign or part of my hieroglyph" (*TF*, 56).

—Albert Gelpi, "Re-Membering the Mother: A Reading of H.D.'s *Trilogy*," *Poesis* 6 (1985): pp. 48–51.

RACHEL BLAU DUPLESSIS ON H.D.'S TRIPLES

[Rachel Blau DuPlessis is a Professor of English at Temple University. She is the author of several books including *Writing Beyond the Ending: Narrative Strategies in Twentieth-Century Women Writers* and *The Pink Guitar: Writing as Feminist Practice*. Here, she examines H.D.'s use of triple images, gained from her vision in Corfu, to reassert female authority in the triad of healing, religion and art.]

True to the triple 'tripod pattern', each of the three epiphanies of Mary in 'Tribute to the Angels' produces or affirms one of the three scientia: healing, religion, art. The pulsing jewel with its iridescent changeable colours in the bottom of the crucible is the figure related to the sciences of alchemy and then medicine, a reinterpreted understanding of the crude, poisonous Venus. The Mary incarnating the May apple flower is the Mary of religion, a rod or rood. And clearly a Mary not as 'the painters' saw her but described anew by a visionary poet is the Mary of art. Each of these Marys is, or carries, one of the emblematic parts of a caduceus: a rod, a quivering jewel, and a blank-bud book with its 'tale of a jar or jars' (*CP*, p. 571).

As the throbbing opalescent jewel, living and perfumed, found by alchemical fusion, its fragrance and shape suggest a milk-filled breast: not only an object of sight, but of physical touch. H.D. focuses her meditation on this jewel, setting words aside, neither naming nor thinking. This symbolic matter suggests it is an anti-bomb: an implosion which shows the same colours and vibrancy as an actual explosion, but to opposite intent, thus an answer to the male serpent Typhoon, god of war. As the flowering may apple from a bomb-charred tree in a vacant lot, Mary is the principle of blossoming incarnate in the damaged historical time after the London Blitz. Again beyond verbalising, more like music, the presentation H.D. makes of this flowered rod is reminiscent of the high revelation of the Eleusinian Mysteries.

The vision of the Lady with her blank book, the third irruption of a mother goddess, the third break in her well-planned narrative celebrating male angels, is a climactic moment of the whole poem because of H.D.'s critique of culture and of poetic stance. Her Mary, as she says, cannot be described citing or conforming to previous iconography. Indeed, the unwritten element of Mary and the unwritten status of her book are powerful statements of female authority. A catalogue (in sections 29–32, then 36–41) of the multifarious depictions of the Madonna in painting, icon and religious doctrine is interspersed with such comments as 'But none of these, none of these/ suggest her as I saw her. . .' and 'she bore/ none of her usual attributes; the Child was not with her' (*CP*, pp. 566–7). Recall that none of the epiphanies uses metaphors of words (one is silent meditation, the next music, the third a blank book): this transcendence of poetry-as-usual has both a spiritual and a feminist dimension.

This new lady 'carries a book but it is not/ the tome of the ancient wisdom,// The pages, I imagine, are the blank pages/ of the unwritten volume of the new . . .' (*CP*, p. 570). H.D.'s blank page of the new is a resistant exploration of the cultural imagery of woman as page awaiting someone else's writing. Because Mary carries a book, not a baby, H.D. proposes the female authority of scribe and law-giver, but unlike the Sibyl 'shut up in a cave', it is not a law in collaboration with (Roman) patriarchy. H.D. offers the possibility that Mary is not a conduit for One whom she bore, but is herself the One: the goddess is God. Further, a woman offers a participatory textual plurality, the virginal page is not single, hieratic, authoritarian revelation. It is the book of prophecy that does not look like a conventional book, from a prophet who does not act like a conventional prophet.

This section, using many small citations from and allusions to Revelations is a proud reconsideration of the absolutism and possessiveness of the prophetic stance. In a parallel to the injunction 'Thou shalt have no other gods before me', John insists that there be no prophets after him. His curse on additions and further witnessing is boldly opposed to the word of Christ who says, 'I make all things new'. H.D. creates a narrative in which the misogynist prophet is proved wrong by both the 'feminine god' and the female prophet.

So in her use of John, H.D. is refabricating not only a misogynist tradition in its casting the Mother Goddess as the enemy of heaven, but all authoritarian voices within that tradition which seal the book. The sealing of the book is a trope for the silencing of women; the blank book is, then, the whiteness of multiplicity, pluralism, and a Christian polytheism; it is the possibility of female gender authority and women's speech.

—Rachel Blau DuPlessis, "Gender Authority." *H.D.The Career of that Struggle* (Bloomington: Indiana University Press, 1986): pp. 92–94.

ALICIA OSTRIKER ON H.D.'S POETICS

[Alicia Ostriker is a Professor of English at Rutgers University. She won the National Book Award for *The Little Space, Poems Selected and New* has written numerous books of poetry and criticism. In this essay, Ostriker explains H.D.'s poetics as innovative and conducive to an open exchange between the reader and the poet.]

In a key lyric of *Tribute to the Angels* (*TA*, 38) we find a subtle play of end-rhymes, some adjacent, some at a distance from each other, underlying the irony of the poet's tone as she responds to her inter-locutor's interpretation of the Lady:

> O yes—you understand, I say,
> this is all most satisfactory,
>
> but she wasn't hieratic, she wasn't frozen,
> she wasn't very tall;
>
> she is the Vestal
> from the days of Numa,
>
> she carries over the cult
> of the *Bona Dea*,
>
> she carries a book but it is not
> the tome of the ancient wisdom,
>
> the pages, I imagine, are the blank pages
> of the unwritten volume of the new;
>
> all you say, is implicit,
> all that and much more;
>
> but she is not shut up in a cave
> like a Sibyl; she is not
>
> imprisoned in leaden bars
> in a coloured window;
>
> she is Psyche, the butterfly,
> out of the cocoon.

Here we have *say/satisfactory*, *tall/Vestal*, *Numa/Bona Dea*, *pages/cave*, and *wisdom/window* as well as *new/dow*, *more/bars*, *not/implicit/not*; and the run of repeated phrases *she wasn't . . . she wasn't . . . she wasn't . . . she is . . . she carries . . . she carries . . . she is not . . . she is not . . . she is.* Repeated sounds, simply as sounds, weave the lyric into a unit. The final two end words *butter-fly* and *cocoon* at the lyric's climax feel to the ear as if they are appropriately outside of any pattern, although butter*fly* faintly but significantly echoes *say* and *satisfactory* and co*coon* significantly echoes fro*zen*.

With a number of exceptions and variations, and with varying degrees of intensity, this is the technique throughout *Trilogy*: there are chains of end-rhymes which may be local or may run through whole lyrics, but which are always inconspicuous and unpredictable in frequency, and which are reinforced by interior sound echoes of all sorts. The reader experiences this, I believe, not as rhyme but (without having to think about it) as beauty and coherence. And this sound-play, I believe, is a formal correlative of the poem's premise that order, beauty, and meaning remain permanently present in our shattered world but not permanently obvious, and that the way to recover them is not through rational effort but through the receptive psychic states of dream and vision which are prior to the semantic Word as the Word is prior to the Sword (*WDNF*, 11, 20). Hearing (without thinking about it) these sound connections is like knowing (below the level of argument) that god exists, that paradise exists. It is precisely this kind of knowledge, softly but firmly opposed to the world of rationalism and violence, to which the poet wishes to lead us. Or, rather, the poet is reminding us of what we already know, of spiritual capacities we already possess. Interpreting her own dream of Osiris as a dream of Christ, she turns to the reader:

> I assure you that the eyes
> Of Velasquez' crucified
>
> now look straight at you,
>> (*WDNF*, 19)

and then turns to further discovery:

> Now it appears very clear
> that the Holy Ghost,
>
> childhood's mysterious enigma
> is the Dream;
>
> that way of inspiration
> is always open
>
> and open to everyone.
> (*WDNF*, 20)

At least part of the magic of H.D. as a poet is her capacity to affirm radically antinomian spiritual principles without theological argument, without rhetoric, merely by creating a pattern of cadences and sounds that perform the work of persuasion. We see what she wants us to see, in part thanks to the complex off-rhymes of "*eyes*" and "cruci*fied*," "ass*ure you*," "cr*u*cified," and again "*you*," the monosyllabic simplicity of "now look straight at you," the play of "app*ears*," "cl*ear*," and "myst*er*ious," "*way*" and "al*ways*," and the quiet assertion through an inconspicuous sound echo of what all churches, schools, scriptures, and orthodoxies are bound to deny: "inspira*tion*," "op*en*," "op*en*," "every*one*."

—Alicia Ostriker, "No Rule of Procedure: The Open Poetics of H.D." Originally in *Agenda* 25 (87–88), reprinted in *Signets: Reading H.D.* (Madison: University of Wisconsin Press, 1990): pp. 342–344.

CLAIRE BUCK ON THE ARTICULATION OF WOMEN'S KNOWLEDGE

[Claire Buck is an Associate Professor of English at Wheaton, College. In this essay, Buck deconstructs the difficulties in articulating woman's knowledge in the construct of a patriarchal language.]

The difference between the idea of something supplementary and something other can be seen in the sequence of lyrics from 36 to 39. Here an imaginary reader interprets the vision in terms of a syncretistic religious tradition, 'This is a symbol of beauty (you continue), / she is Our Lady universally'. The poet does not reject these interpretations but writes that 'all you say; is implicit, / all that and much more' (*TA*, 103). The definitions that follow define her as escaping:

> she is not
>
> imprisoned in leaden bars
> in a coloured window;
>
> she is Psyche, the butterfly,
> out of the cocoon.
>
> (*TA*, 103)

However, even the affirmative definition 'she is Psyche' is given the same provisionality as the standard cultural representations which imprison her 'in leaden bars'. The lyric which follows opens with the qualifier 'But', and a series of definitions which investigate the question of definition in relation to the cultural tradition and the terms of representation. Her definition in lyric 39 is relational: 'nearer than Guardian Angel', 'counter-coin-side / of primitive terror', and by means of negatives which are themselves substantives:

> she is not-fear, she is not-war,
> but she is no symbolic figure
>
> of peace, charity, chastity, goodness
> faith, hope, reward.
> (*TA*, 104)

The symbols bind her back into the terms and tradition which H.D. is challenging and which therefore have to be rejected. But her vision of the Lady can only be posed in relation to that tradition of imagery. The story which the poet imagines in the book 'written or unwritten' and the figure of the lady are 'the same—different—the same attributes, / different yet the same as before' (*TA*, 105). The repetition here represents the poet's predicament, that the different is only different by virtue of its difference from the dominant term which is the problem. An alternative order of difference of the kind posed by Cixous is not here in question. But the repetition also undermines the concept of the original, 'the same' from which H.D.'s vision differs, because it insists on the necessary relation between the same and the different, the 'same' requires the difference to define it.

H.D.'s strategy of dramatising the difficulty of definition, rather than the vision itself, also registers the impossibility of simply leaving behind the aesthetic and cultural inheritance on which *Trilogy* leans. She writes:

> This is no rune nor symbol,
> what I mean is—it is so simple
>
> yet no trick of the pen or brush
> could capture that impression;
> (*TA*, 106)

and 'What I wanted to indicate', 'when I said white, / I did not mean' and 'what can we say?'. This is like T.S. Eliot's 'intolerable wrestle with words and meanings', although *Four Quartets*, influential as it was on *Trilogy*, never explicitly links the issue of the limits of representation to sexual difference. H.D. also uses an either/or structure as in lyric 41,

> She carried a book, *either* to imply
> she was one of us, with us,
>
> *or* to suggest she was satisfied
> with our purpose, a tribute to the Angels,
> > (*TA*, 107; my emphasis)

with the result that the vision is represented as irreducible to its interpretation and meaning.

This is apparent in the final lyric 43, where a resolution is represented: 'when we gain / the arc of perfection' (*TA*, 109). The resolution uses an alchemical motif which runs through 'Tribute to the Angels' to suggest that the poem's achievement is a transformation of the cultural tradition which defines the woman:

> but when the jewel
> melts in the crucible,
>
> we find not ashes, not ash-of-rose,
> not a tall vase and a staff of lilies,
>
> not *vas spirituale*,
> not *rosa mystica* even,
>
> but a cluster of garden-pinks
> or a face like a Christmas-rose.
> > (*TA*, 109–10)

The jewel in the crucible appears earlier as what the poet cannot name, in lyrics 13 and 14. Here it turns out to be the lady, redefined and bringing resurrection 'we rise again from death and live'. However, even here where the vision is defined according to the conventional theological symbols, such as the lilies and the Roman Catholic Laurentian Litany to the Virgin, that definition repeats the either/or structure: 'a cluster . . . or a face like . . .'. The formula resists definition and interpretation at the same time that it represents the vision. Even the use of a simile contributes to this resistance by stressing the play of similarity and difference at the heart of representation. The identification is only possible because she is not like, different from. Something is again left over. As Rachel Blau DuPlessis says about the book with blank pages which the Lady carries, H.D.'s image 'is a resistant exploration of the cultural imagery of woman as page awaiting someone else's writing'.

This 'resistant exploration' does however also produce its own representation of femininity. A content emerges out of H.D.'s critical re-examination of tradition. One of the meanings which defines the Lady, and hence femininity, is that she is indefinable—something about her escapes or resists definition. She is also figured as different, other and even represented by negation, 'not-fear'. These categories then become part of H.D.'s representation of femininity. Arguably the poem avoids the potential trap by which these categories repeat a familiar representation of femininity as a form of otherness that supports a masculine arrogation of a full subjectivity. Although the unrepresentability and otherness of the woman in *Trilogy* threaten to leave her outside both language and history, H.D.'s critique of a western theological and artistic tradition acts to refuse the universalising claims of that tradition. It is not that femininity is outside language, but that it cannot be represented in the terms of that tradition except as its support. The definition of femininity which emerges out of *Trilogy*'s 'resistant exploration', femininity as something which escapes representation, promises that femininity is not simply reducible to its inscription within a patriarchal tradition. There is more to be said, I want to argue, however, that this promise remains problematic in *Trilogy* because the poem identifies the unrepresentable residue as a truth located in individual experience. The way in which the poem establishes the value and significance of individual experience defines the knowledge produced by that experience in opposition to representation. But the relationship of representation to the female subject is at the core of *Trilogy*'s investigation of tradition. Thus there is a difficulty in grounding knowledge of the woman in personal experience when the very issue of how we define the personal and subjective is at stake. I will now go on to examine the process by which *Trilogy* links the unrepresentable to the category of the experiential and the implications of this move.

—Claire Buck, "'She can not know that she knows this': Woman's Knowledge." *H.D. and Freud: Bisexuality and Feminine Discourse.*, (New York: Harverster Wheatsheaf, 1991): pp. 136–139.

Brenda Hillman on H.D.'s "Lady"

[Brenda Hillman teaches poetry writing at St. Mary's College in California. She has several books of poetry and has received a Guggenheim Foundation Fellowship, two Pushcart Prizes and the Delmore Schwarts Memorial Award for Poetry. Hillman explores the failures in the characterization of H.D.'s Lady, their effect on the overall reading of the poem and on Hillman as a poet.]

The second thing I found was that H.D. attempts to reveal, rather than to conjure, an absolute metaphysical weirdness. Here I look to the second of *Trilogy*'s meditations, "Tribute to the Angels." The poem doesn't reject its own pluralism while assembling the apparatus for an essentially feminist vision. I love her weirdness. In a stiff—you could almost say nude-*with-clothes-on*,-descending-the-staircase—image she brings the Lady into the poem after covering a lot of spiritual mileage, from Hermes, to John, to angels and Mary, going from figure to figure as if visiting relatives in small midwestern towns, plain-ness, no antics, but also no sentimentality. If in her descriptions of buildings she gets to use exotic solids like jasper and lapis, she seems to go for the stripped-down deity, and thus the Lady comes almost as plain vanilla, the multipurpose goddess figure with many artists' hands laying a touch here and there. This figure has without a doubt had a huge impact an my work—and not just mine, the work of many other writers, including Duncan and Barbara Guest. In admiring H.D.'s stew of gods and spiritual presences, I learned that the human imagination, when it confronts what it might think of as god-ness, metaphysical abstraction, or even traditional religious iconography, doesn't have to be the agent of an impossible narrowness that we usually associate with belief. Another way of saying this is that she allowed me to go deeper and be strange, even inconsistent, in a worldview I felt I had inherited from inward traditions of American Protestantism and all the Western occult and esoteric traditions that had laced it like swirls of chocolate in marble fudge. H.D., quite simply, gave a sense about what needed to be remade.

What was most instructive about this figure of the Lady as I encountered her for the first time, marching slowly down, was that H.D. was enacting a revision of the visionary method. The figure of the Lady, appearing in her joyous, teasing, sort of sexy-mommy mood as Psyche, the anima, imagination, Venus, Aphrodite, you name it, carries the Book of Possibility, and this development of the goddess snatched simultaneously from tradition and personal sources is legible as a figure for the artist in our time. The dream comes in the middle. We want Gabriel but we get the Lady who steps down canyons, the one whom we cannot hold, ever, but who gives us everything. I was enchanted by the state of delirium H.D. described; it coincided with some experiences of reverie I had had in which an unnamed figure comes simultaneously as a helper and as a muse but who maybe turned into a pet image, the way a painted Mexican mask that has been carved by a single hand to reinvent a single soul may also appeal to the generalized need.

The problem I encountered with this figure—this is my com- plaint—is the humorlessness and the occasional sanctimoniousness of the sacred one and of the speaker's relationship to her—not so much the polemical earnestness of the whole routine since, as I say, I had bought the nine-island cruise package early on, recognizing that H.D. works in circles of symbolic possibility. But writing like

> We see her visible and actual,
> beauty incarnate,
>
> as no high-priest of Astoroth
> could compel her
>
> with incense
> and potent spell;
>
> we asked for no sign
> but she gave a sign unto us; (1973: 82)

makes me just want to jab my finger in H.D.'s swooning middle and say, "Stop fakin' it, girl, let's go outside and smoke." The weighti- ness in general—and in specific—of all the arcane presentation, however forceful and amazing it can be, of one figure after another makes me laugh. almost in the same way that watching certain rock videos in hotel rooms makes me laugh, not exactly with a snort but just with an "uh, yeah, right," though when rock videos are humorless it's exactly because they can reflect an awareness of how absurd the initial propositions are, and this is not a bit true of H.D.; she makes a reader wish the decor of the fairly tacky sublime were not so unironically gaudy and that there were a lot more displays of antic shame, or at least that the invisible that is promised had a few more tattoos of lizards and snakes.

Probably responding, to the humorlessness and grandiosity was part of my purpose in *Death Tractates*. In many metaphors of religious rescue, the soteriological figures leave the rescued one with the nausea of intense longing even while arriving thoroughly; responding to *Trilogy*'s weightiness, though I admired its oracular dualism, I devised a speaker who makes asides and hesitates and makes a few jokes while she gives up having a "satisfying" relationship to the spirit world she so craves. The saviors function in a daily way rather than existing in a heaven the speaker believes exists and can't reach; this quotidian, with all its DMV papers and camellias and library slots and mockingbirds, keeps the lost body in the world as a paratactic accomplice of yearning. I don't suppose my vision is any more or less dualistic than H.D.'s, for all that, but I'm interested in the erotic besideness of the other in a different way, perhaps because it's cozier and sillier and more remote. Possibly writing about the spirit world can never be funny enough if the job for the first half of life is to grieve the passing of everything. I don't know what the main job for the second half is, quite yet. I suspect it's more fun.

—Brenda Hillman, "Three Thoughts on *Trilogy*." *H.D. and Poets After*. (Iowa City: University of Iowa Press, 2000): pp. 187–189.

EILEEN GREGORY ON POET AS WITNESS

[In this extract, Gregory compares the poetry of Carolyn Forché with that of H.D., claiming that both act as witness in times of extremity.]

At one point in "Tribute to the Angels," the speaker attempts to convey a visionary moment prompted by an actual event. Here she is called up short by an image that resists the figural: among the ruins, "a charred tree . . . burnt and stricken to the heart" but blossoming:

> This is no rune nor riddle,
> it is happening everywhere;
>
> what I mean is—it is so simple
> yet no trick of the pen or brush
>
> could capture that impression;
> music could do nothing with it,
>
> nothing whatever; what I mean is—
> but you have seen for yourself
>
> that burnt-out wood crumbling . . .
> you have seen for yourself. (*H.D.*, 1983: 559)

The insistence, "This is no rune nor riddle," calls attention to another kind of sign, a part of the given. The literal image will not go beyond itself: its significance is not representable, and it is only "readable" by others who share in this condition of extremity. The reader is indeed suddenly confronted with the burden of witnessing: "you have seen for yourself." In the next section the poet tries to articulate this untranslatable quality:

> . . . music? O, what I meant
> by music when I said music, was—
>
> music sets up ladders,
> it makes us invisible,
>
> it sets us apart,
> it lets us escape;
>
> but from the visible
> there is no escape;
>
> there is no escape from the spear
> that pierces the heart. (*H.D.*, 1983: 559–60)

In this confrontation the poet in a sense defines the dislocation involved in reading a historical marker: one instinct is to draw away from the image through representation (as "music sets up ladders . . .

lets us escape"), but the image rooted in a historical circumstance remains intractable ("from the visible / there is no escape"). Moreover, that image—both for the poet who confronts it here and for the reader—opens a wound ("the spear / that pierces the heart"), clearly one carrying the memory of repeated violence and devastation. H.D.'s poem marks this moment and marks the reader.

Besides the presence of this figure, *Trilogy* and *The Angel of History* share other emphases in common with poetry of witness. The opening section of "The Walls Do Not Fall" suggests some of these in its extended parallel of the ruined houses of London with the ruins of Karnak and Pompeii and with the ruined house of body and soul. The predominant image of the ruined city in both poems is a metonym for the devastation of history. H.D. traces out distant historical parallels for the besieged and destroyed city, the "smouldering cities" of Pompeii, Jerusalem, Thebes, Rome. Forché's record of lost cities is more immediate:

> If a city, ruin, if an animal, hunger.
> If a grave, anonymous.
> If a century, this. (1994: 6)

But these are the ruins, too, of one's own history: "The past is not where you left it, Svetko. /It is a ruined city, spackled with grief" (Forché 1994: 39). The poet in "The Walls Do Not Fall" catalogs that personal devastation, the careening path of "an erratic burnt-out comet" (H.D. 1983: 535), and *The Angel of History* begins with the image of "a woman broken into many women" (*Forché*, 1994: 3). Within this ruin, the poem, Forché claims, becomes an "excavation site," like those of Karnak and Pompeii.

A third implication of ruin suggested in H.D.'s poem is a crucial part of the record in *The Angel of History*. The bombs slice open buildings, exposing the intimate space of human habitation: "the fallen roof / leaves the sealed room / open to the air," and, going through the streets,

> . . . we pass on
>
> to another cellar, to another sliced wall
> where poor utensils show
> like rare objects in a museum; (*H.D.*, 1983: 509–10)

Conditions of extremity shatter ordinary human habitation, objectify what is exposed, making what was part of a living fabric of life into a specimen. This exposure of fragile life points to a general emphasis in H.D.'s poem upon the ordinary and vulnerable as focal sites of significance; indeed, the comparison of the unsealed London houses with the roofless temple insists upon the ordinary as a sacred sphere. Forché's poem persistently renders this dimension of loss. The familiar is almost obliterated:

> This is what we have taken the ordinary world to mean:
> bootprints in clay,
> the persistence of tracked field.
>
> What was there before imperfectly erased
>   and memory a reliquary in a wall of silence.
>   (*Forché*, 1994: 44)

The past remains in isolated images, painful in marking not only an unspoken catastrophe but the loss of a shared human world: "A wedding dress hanging in a toolshed outside Warsaw" (Forché 1994: 19). In the context of this erased life, the longing that comes in memory is "the defenselessness for which there is no cure" (Forché 1994: 43, 65).

—Eileen Gregory, "H.D. and Carolyn Forché" *H.D. and Poets After.* (Iowa City: University of Iowa Press, 2000): pp. 274–276.

"The Flowering of the Rod"

"The Flowering of the Rod" finishes *Trilogy*, bringing resolution to the creation of a resolute faith in the Word created in "The Walls Do Not Fall" and defended as equal between the genders based on syncretist visions in "Tribute to the Angels." Here, H.D. forces the patriarchy to re-vision Mary Magdalene as the Virgin Mary, suggesting that the sacred exists as powerfully in women as it does in men and that purity lies in the soul and not the body. In fact, it is H.D.'s claim that the two need not be mutually exclusive. It also expresses a jubilant feeling that the first two poems do not possess. The Second World War is coming to an end, the artist has emerged from the chrysalis invoked in "The Walls Do Not Fall" and the prospect of a rebuilding and revamping of the world order excited H.D. and her language reflects that.

The poem opens with the narrator shifting her attention from surviving to rebuilding. Instead of pity for the dead, she believes the populace needs to find love, the highest attainment of spiritual wisdom. She accepts this hermetic wisdom and the jewel of the sacred wisdom created in "Tribute to the Angels." Ultimately, utter destruction has not been wrought; the poet knows that ". . .ultimately we will find// happiness." Still, in the midst of happiness, there are those who have found Paradise and want to go back. Rather than simply resting after the war's end, they work resolutely to regain Paradise. The poet becomes a part of that group, working to bear witness and construct a new notion of the sacred, much as Imagism and Modernism created new notions of writing. This poem reacts against traditional notions of faith and modes of writing.

H.D. writes:

> what men say is-not—I remember,
> I remember, I remember—you have forgot;
> you think, even before it is half-over,
> that your cycle is at an end.

She returns to her assertion from "The Walls Do Not Fall," this war is a chrysalis stage, to strengthen and mature the artist so that she might bring resurrection to the world when the destruction is over.

Though both destruction and resurrection exist, men only give primacy to destruction. Christ, in his incarnation as man, and Kaspar are the exception to this rule.

In the eleventh stanza, H.D. characterizes Christ as an individual who comes in after the destruction. He befriends the whore, the leper, the thief. To all, he brings ressurection and Mary Magdalene is among them. Traditionally depicted as whore, H.D. chooses another vision for the character of Mary. In this vision, Mary is a prophet, a repository for the sacred. She is neither virgin nor whore; H.D. does not let these societal identities typify the character. She moves to a characterization representative of the soul, something which traditional patriarchal characterizations denied the character. Mary Magdalene meets and strikes a bargain with Kaspar, one of the three Magi to visit the Christ child. This particular Magi comes from Arabic lands and brings with him the perfume of myrrh, a name that means "bitter' in Arabic, due to its scent. The plant shares its word origins with Mary, creating for H.D. a seeming lexical inevitability.

Mary comes to the market to find Kaspar, to demand from him the gift of myrrh, so that she might wash the feet of Christ. Initially, Kaspar tries to dismiss her twice, but Mary closes the door behind him, sealing them both in his house. As she stands with her back to the door, barring him from leaving, her scarf falls to the floor, leaving her hair unbound. Kaspar begins to judge her, thinking her overbold to come into the house of a stranger and to be found with her hair unbound. It is unseemly. Thankfully, a vision derails his limited and traditional view. In her hair, he begins to see light and then a vision of Paradise as the Hersperides and Atlantis. He sees the plan for the world unfolding in the simplest things, grains of sand, flecks and specks. He envisions a world prior to Adam, one in which men and women are equal. It is to this paradise that the poet strives. She creates Kaspar and Mary as ultimately equal partners in bringing the sacred to Christ. H.D. perpetuates this idea by allowing Kaspar to see a jewel, presumably the same jewel created in "Tribute to the Angels" when Hermes melts the jasper and when the Lady visits the poet. This jewel represents the power of the sacred. Before Kaspar can relate this vision or reconcile it, Mary leaves his home, claiming there is nothing he can give her. After she departs, he contrives to give the myrrh to her, realizing that she already carries the sacred scent, that the sacred is an experience. This myrrh also acts in a cyclical nature of multiple proportions. First, throughout his life, Christ receives myrrh: at his birth, at a dinner wherein Mary Magdalene washes his feet and at his death. Kaspar knows the cycle of myrrh from bringing it to Christ and from his visions of Mary. The poet uses the symbol of myrrh to reinforce the idea of history's cycle and the attention it must be paid.

The poem continues illustrating the historical, mythopoetic cycle when Mary receives the myrrh and takes it to wash the feet of Christ. The act harkens back to the Philosopher's Stone because this scent can bring forgiveness and resurrection, sharing a sort of spiritual alchemy with the stone. It becomes, in essence, the elixir of life, so that Christ might rise again, giving woman an integral rule in the continuation of the divine. Mary washes his feet with her unbound hair, alarming both Judas and the leper, Simon. They represent the patriarchy, men made uneasy by a woman's show of sensuality and of power. They claim to not know her, to find her indecent. Throughout the poem, and the sections that precede it, H.D. suggests that a woman's power strikes fear in men and for this reason, has been suppressed. She believes the result of any suppression leaves people destined to repeat that which they suppress, again enacting a cycle of sublimation and recovery. Both Christ and Mary become compelling examples of this phenomenon.

Ultimately though, Kaspar's voice finishes the poem. After he gave the myrrh to Mary, he began to wonder what made his vision possible. Was it a belief in the repetition of history? Was it destiny? Is it explicable through words or mathematics? Like H.D., he comes to believe that his knowledge is pre-history, stemming from some primordial knowledge, impossible to articulate, a knowledge grounded in experience, a true knowledge as posited earlier in the sequence. In the final stanza, H.D. returns the cycle to the Magi in the manger. In the midst of the scene, a woman sits "shy and simple and young," nothing like the serene beauty created by Western culture. She speaks to Kaspar, thanking him for his gift, "a most beautiful fragrance,/ as of all flowering things together." In this final vision of history, Kaspar comes to see Mary as the Lady of H.D.'s vision in "Tribute to the Angels" and he comes to understand that the fragrance that Mary claims to smell seeps not from the jar, but from the sacred bundle in her arms. In this final stanza, the hermetic jewel becomes myrrh and the Christ Child. The Lady becomes Mary Magdalene and the Virgin Mother. The sacred passes continually through the hands of males and females in an endless cycle of destruction and resurrection. The poet becomes scribe and prophet of a new, more democratic notion of the divine that spans centuries and mythologies. The quest begun in "The Walls Do Not Fall" finds fulfillment of its cycle in "The Flowering of the Rod."

"The Flowering of the Rod"

ADALAIDE MORRIS ON THEORIES OF PROJECTION

[Adalaide Morris is Professor of English at the University
of Iowa. She is the author of *Wallace Stevens: Imagination
and Faith* and a co-editor of *Extended Outlooks: The Iowa
Review Collection of Contemporary Women Writers.* Here,
she explains the way in which images project to the
poet/visionary who in turn projects them to an audience,
thereby creating a link between the sacred and reality.]

In "The Flowering of the Rod," part three of *Trilogy*, the crucible is
not a place or a poem but the legend of resurrection: "a tale of a
Fisherman, / a tale of a jar or jars," an ancient story which in its
Christian form is "the same—different—the same attributes, / different yet the same as before" (*T*, 105). What the poet-alchemist
must break down here is the familiar racist and misogynist reading
of the scriptures that dismisses Kaspar as a dark heathen and Mary
Magdalene as a devil-ridden harlot, making both peripheral to the
real story. In H.D.'s rewriting, they are central. The first two parts of
Trilogy had precipitated a new male and female principle; now, in
part three, they meet in alchemical marriage to effect the miraculous
transformation. Kaspar, who might be Abraham or an Angel or even
God (*T*, 140), is here a somewhat forgetful and fallible philosopher,
dream-interpreter, astrologer, and alchemist from a long line of
Arabs who knew "the secret of the sacred processes of distillation"
(*T*, 133). He carries with him a sealed jar of myrrh exuding a fra-
grance that is the eternal essence "of all flowering things together"
(*T*, 172): the elixir of life, the seed of resurrection.

Kaspar was traveling to "a coronation and a funeral," like all
alchemical transmutations "a double affair" (*T*, 130), when found by
Mary Magdalene, avatar of H.D.'s "mer, mere, mère, mater, Maia,
Mary, // Star of the Sea, / Mother." When he momentarily abandons
his patriarchal stiffness and, assuming a posture of reverence, stoops
to pick up Mary's scarf, he is granted a vision that reaches back to

"the islands of the Blest" and "the lost centre-island, Atlantis" (*T*, 153) and forward to "the whole scope and plan // of our and his civilization on this, / his and our earth" (*T*, 154). The spell he hears recovers the lost matriarchal genealogy, identifies Mary as heritor of "*Lilith born before Eve / and one born before Lilith, / and Eve*" (*T*, 157, italics in original), and convinces Kaspar to yield her the precious myrrh. This act—in H.D.'s astonishing rewriting—seeds the resurrection. When Mary washes the feet of Christ, she anoints him with the elixir of life and insures that his crucifixion will be the first step in triumphant regeneration. Consecrated by Mary, Christ himself becomes the legendary philosopher's stone: the resurrection and the life.

Mary Magdalene's washing of the feet of Christ is the act of the alchemist: the projecting of the Mage's elixir onto substance prepared for transmutation. Behind the story of Kaspar and Mary is the old tale of sulphur and mercury; ahead of it is the work of the poet-alchemist who wanted to give us, through her combinations and recombinations of lost spells and legends, the power to transmute our own damaged civilization. The ultimate, audacious hope of *Trilogy* is that it might itself become an elixir of life, a resurrective power.

—Adalaide Morris, "The Concept of Projection." *Contemporary Literature* 25 (Winter 1984): pp. 434–435.

DONNA KROLIK HOLLENBERG ON FREUD AS MUSE

[Here Hollenberg posits that H.D. transformed herself into her own child and recovered her own female power, thereby transforming Freud from master to muse.]

Similarly, in "The Flowering of the Rod" H.D. transforms Freud from a master into a muse. In a series of dramatic episodes that alludes to central issues of her analysis as well as to the gospels, H.D. reminds us that the first to witness Christ's "life-after-death" was "an unbalanced, neurotic woman" who was "out of step with world so-called progress" (*T*, 129). A fusion of Mary of Bethany (who disavowed housework) and the "reviled" Mary Magdalen, she also becomes associated with the Madonna in the revised nativity scene with which H.D. concludes the *Trilogy*. Leading up to this epiphany is an imaginative re-creation of how Mary Magdalen acquires the precious jar of myrrh with which she anoints the feet of Christ.

In H.D.'s version Mary receives the contents of the alabaster jar as a gift from the merchant Kaspar after an amusing scene in the Arab bazaar that is a comic transposition of her own encounter with Freud. Like the old professor (who had felt "the fangs of the pack" as a Jew in Vienna), Kaspar is no ordinary entrepreneur but a "stranger in the marketplace"; his "priceless" burial spice is "not for sale" (*T*, 130). A philosopher-alchemist who knows the "secret of the sacred processes of distillation," he is taking it to a "coronation and a funeral—a double affair" (*T*, 133, 130). Also something of a male chauvinist, Kaspar snubs Mary at first, fixing his eyes on the half-open door "in a gesture of implied dismissal" after she ignores his insulting sexual overtures (*T*, 131). Here H.D. burlesques Freud's phallocentrism. When Kaspar draws aside his robe "in a noble manner," the "unmaidenly" Mary does not "take the hint" (*T*, 130). Having seen "nobility herself at first hand," she is not impressed (*T*, 130). Simply detaching herself, she firmly holds her ground and finally leaves on her own terms: "I am Mary, a great tower; / through my will and my power, / Mary shall be myrrh" (*T*, 135).

Yet, though he has been conditioned to think that it is "unseemly" for a woman to "appear disordered, dishevelled," Kaspar is struck by Mary's unpredictability. And when he momentarily abandons his patriarchal stiffness, bending down in a posture of reverence to pick up the scarf that has slipped from her hair, he is granted a vision that complements the poet's own. For unlike the Christian Simon the leper, who later derides Mary as "devil-ridden" because he fears her lack of inhibition, the heathen Kaspar recognizes that she embodies the once-revered female deities of a prebiblical period. Realizing that they are "unalterably part of the picture," he "might call // the devils *daemons*", invoking them tenderly "under his breath . . . without fear of eternal damnation":

> Isis, Astarte, Cyprus
> and the other four;

he might re-name them,
Ge-meter, De-meter, earth-mother

or Venus
in a star. (*T*, 145)

When Mary's scarf slips to the floor, Kaspar recognizes that she represents "Venus in the ascendant // or Venus in conjunction with Jupiter" (*T*, 148). Here is the poetic counterpart to H.D.'s culminating vision at Corfu, in which an ascendant Niké is drawn into the sundisk by a welcoming male figure.

In that half-second, when his intuition is in "direct contradiction" with the "hedges and fences and fortresses" of his thought (*T*, 159, 158), Kaspar has an experience that echoes the speaker's earlier vision of the Lady and recalls the luminous Princess dream of the Freud memoir. He sees that the light from Mary's hair is "as of moonlight on a lost river" and he remembers (*T*, 148). Through a fleck of light in the jeweled crown of the tripartite goddess who appears to his inner eye, Kaspar sees backward to the "islands of the Blest" and "the lost centre-island, Atlantis," and he sees forward to "the whole scope and plan // of our and his civilization on this, / his and our earth, before Adam" (*T*, 153, 154). This vision leads him, along with the poet, to hear an extremely important message.

Like "the echo of an echo in a shell," which does not conform to any known words but conveys itself rhythmically, the spell Kaspar hears reminds him of "the drowned cities of pre-history" as it translates itself (*T*, 156). Implying that a matriarchal genealogy has been erased from record, it recalls an ancient female trinity that suggests a condition of female potential quite different from that of Genesis:

> *Lilith born before Eve*
> *and one born before Lilith*
> *and Eve; we three are forgiven,*
> *we are three of the seven*
> *daemons cast out of her.* (*T*, 157)

Created not from Adam's rib but from the dust, Lilith was a woman who refused sexual subordination and dared to pronounce the Ineffable Name. As Susan Gubar has written, she and the unnamed daemon actually predate the Bible, establishing a link back to Kaspar's pagan deities: "together they promise a submerged but now recoverable time of female strength, female speech and female sexuality, all of which have mysteriously managed to survive, although in radically subdued ways, incarnate in the body of Mary Magdala." Like Freud, who compared his new understanding of the preoedipal phase of female development to the discovery of Mycenean civilization behind Greece, Kaspar is a healer, a shaman of sorts. By recapturing Mary's "stolen soul, her lost ancestors," he reestablishes "the matriarchal genealogy that confers divinity upon her."

After the Arab merchant Kaspar has apprehended the full nature of Mary Magdalen, he is transformed into the Mage worthy of the epiphany in the final sections. Dramatically reversing the chronology of his life, H.D. turns backward from his confrontation with this Mary to reinterpret his delivery of the gift of myrrh to Mary in the manger. When Kaspar places his jar on the stable floor, he has a premonition that "there were always two jars, / the two were always together," and he vows *someday I will bring the other*" (*T*, 168). When Kaspar remembers that there were two jars originally together, H.D. alludes to the legendary jar of spikenard that was believed to have magical properties because it contained Christ's circumcised foreskin. The "other jar" that Kaspar will bring someday contains a substance that is the male counterpart of female reproductive power: in the lore of magic, myrrh was credited with the power to cause menstruation. But we already know that his wish has been or will be fulfilled. For when Kaspar gives the myrrh to Mary mother, the poet has already informed us that he is destined to give the other jar to Mary Magdalen.

Finally both Marys recede from the foreground of the poem. For in the closing epiphany of this revised nativity scene, Kaspar's celebration of "the Holy-Presence-Manifest" refers not simply to the child in Mary's lap but to the speaker's recentering, to the appearance "in-herself" that her speech and virginal demeanor imply: "But she spoke so he looked at her, / she was shy and simple and young" (*T*, 168). Realizing that she herself contains the mystery of her transformed sorrow, he wonders if she knows that the "beautiful fragrance" she acknowledges comes not from his sealed jar but from "the bundle of myrrh" she holds in her arms (*T*, 170). In this final vision, which alludes to the Song of Songs, Kaspar finds manifest the triumph of eros over death.

This fragrant bundle of myrrh in the arms of the revived speaker at the end of *Trilogy* recalls the sprig of orange blossom H.D. received from Freud one winter day during her analysis, one of the concluding memories recorded in *Writing on the Wall*. Both represent the poet's conversion of Aaron's rod to a female symbol: to a goldenrod, to a golden bough "with its cluster of golden fruit" (*TF*, 90). Both signify her recovery and ownership of the indwelling spirit of fertility. For H.D.'s changed attitude toward authoritative men, facilitated in analysis, culminated in reconnection with her mother, with herself as imaginal child, and with her dream of prophecy in poetry. Reinventing Freud in her memoir, she made him a muse instead of a master. As a poetic complement to that tribute, she appears in "The Flowering" restored to herself.

> —Donna Krolik Hollenberg, "Creating the Imaginal Child: Freud and 'The Flowering of the Rod.'" *H.D.: The Poetics of Childbirth and Creativity*, (Boston: Northeastern University Press, 1991): pp. 135–139.

HELEN SWORD ON GENDER-BENDING AND PROPHECY

[In this extract, Sword discusses the way in which H.D. reconfigures mythic figures to create a hermaphroditic god(dess) who possesses the sacred.]

Throughout *Trilogy*, as in her earlier poetry, H.D. invokes many outside sources of inspiration, including not only "Apollo, . . . Lord of Magic and Prophecy and Music," and Athene, "the grey-eyed Goddess," but also a wide range of heterodox religious figures, from the Egyptian Amen-Ra to the Christian Virgin Mary to a series of apocryphal angels. Yet she also frees herself of any real dependence on such figures by emphasizing her own creative and interpretive autonomy. Specifically, she takes on for herself the hermeneutic and hermetic functions, respectively, of Hermes, who translates (in the word's etymological sense of "carrying over") divine messages to humankind, and of Hermes Trismegistus, the ancient alchemist whose ability to transform ordinary substances into gold H.D. figures as emblematic of the poet's craft.

Like Hermes Trismegistus, "thrice-master" of magic, astrology, and alchemy, or the Delphic Pythia, whose three-legged tripod represents the fusion of religion, art, and medicine in prophetic utterance, H.D. tries, in her three-part *Trilogy*, to transcend bipolar dualities by breaking them into more complex yet ultimately more stable units of three. Invoking powerful figures from both male and female prophetic and religious traditions (Samuel, John of Patmos, Christ; the Pythia, the Virgin Mary, Mary Magdalen), she offers herself as an Athene-like hermaphroditic figure who, speaking with the voices of both sexes, charts a new path of heterodox prophecy between them. While she does not seek to overthrow traditional male–female stereotypes, H.D. merges them together in new, doubly potent symbolic combinations; for instance, with the "Flowering of the Rod" that serves as an image for London's rebirth from the ashes of war, she collapses male–female symbolic hierarchies by crowning with flowers, symbols of female sexuality, a phallic staff associated with the male prophet Aaron. The flowering rod, which in the Old Testament marks Aaron's ordination as a priest and later helps Moses bring forth water from the desert, has always symbolized both special selection and fertility, but only within a purely patriarchal tradition; indeed, D. H. Lawrence exploits the masculinist elements of the image in his 1922 novel *Aaron's Rod*, the title of which refers to the protagonist's flute (and hence to his powers as artist) but also to his phallic self-sufficiency. H.D., in contrast, emphasizes the rod's hermaphroditic element: permutating *rod* into *rood* and thence to "the flowering of the reed," she unites images of precision (rod and reed are biblical instruments of measurement) and emotion (the reed symbolizes music and thereby poetry), thus bringing together a further set of bipolar opposites (logos/pathos) in a single figure for prophetic power.

—Helen Sword, "H.D. and the Poetics of Possession." *Engendering Inspiration: Visionary Strategies in Rilke, Lawrence and H.D.* (Ann Arbor: University of Michigan Press, 1995): pp. 159–160.

[Here, Laity discusses the way in which H.D. reclaims the
abject bodies of females and the notion of the femme fatale,
recovering power for the female body as the site of both the
sacred and the sexual.]

> lo, her wonderfully woven hair!
> —Swinburne, "Laus Veneris"

Kaspar's induction into a feminist vision of prehistory and a "paradise" of the new Eve, turns on a central (male) Romantic and modern trope for the stranglehold of female sexuality—the Pre-
Raphaelite femme fatale's luxuriant, overflowing hair. *The
Flowering of the Rod's* femme fatale, Mary Magdalene, popularly
believed to be a prostitute cast out for adultery and an exiled wan-
derer in the desert, forms the heroic prototype of *Trilogy's* female
deject-prophets. H.D.'s "other Mary" retains rather than expels
Magdalene's legendary "demons," renamed "*daemons*," who are
revised to include the reclaimed Venusian femme fatale—"Venus/in
a star" (*CP* 25; 595, 596). However, as the narrative makes clear,
Magdalene's transforming *daemons* reside in her "extraordinary
hair," whose visionary depths provide a luminous gateway into
Kaspar's final vision of a prophesied feminine world. Kaspar's
seduction begins with the provocation of Magdalene's unveiled,
untamed hair, which excites him to brand her variously as "unseemly," "disheveled," "unmaidenly," and "disordered." Although her
pale face and luminous eyes command attention, her hair irritates
and diverts him: "But eyes? he had known many women— / it was
her hair un-maidenly— // it was hardly decent of her to stand there,
/ unveiled, in the house of a stranger" (16; 590). The fantastic lure of
Magdalene's glowing hair, however, soon resurfaces in his desperate
longings and hallucinatory images "as of moon-light on a lost river
/ or a sunken stream, seen in a dream // by a parched, dying man, lost
in the desert . . . / or a mirage . . . It was her hair" (17; 591; ellipses
H.D.'s). Reverently, he later watches Magdalene at a social gathering "deftly un-weaving // the long, carefully-braided tresses / of her
extraordinary hair" (21; 594). Simon, the host, warns him to resist

the spell of her hair, comparing her to a "siren" he had seen in "a heathen picture, or a carved stone-portal entrance to a forbidden sea temple":

> they called the creature,
> depicted like this
>
> seated on the sea-shore
> or on a rock, a Siren,
>
> a maid-of-the sea, a mermaid;
> some said, this mermaid sang
>
> and that a Siren-song was fatal
> and wrecks followed the wake of such hair

Kaspar, nevertheless, is drawn more deeply into the siren discourse, until he yields, entirely en-tranced: Reflected light on Magdalene's hair recasts it as a visionary body that draws him into an infinite regress of mirrors and "flecks" of light, "through spiral upon spiral of the shell / of memory that yet connects us // with the drowned cities of pre-history" to a "Paradise before Eve" (32, 33; 603, 602).

Magdalene's wild hair joins *Trilogy*'s cascade of writhing, devouring, imploding bodies even as it draws directly on the famous Pre-Raphaelite trope. Its revised Medusan affect—Magdalene's hair inspires rather than stymies vision—once more reclaims the sexual, creative powers of the Pre-Raphaelite femme fatale, known for her magic hair. Indeed, H.D.'s portrayal of Magdalene's hair may have derived directly from Rossetti's portrait of the "other" Eve, *Lady Lilith*, combing her magnificent swath of hair. While the marbled androgynous boys and Artemisian women of H.D.'s earlier work were not notable for their hair, references to the "mermaid on the rocks" combing her hair or to "Venus in the looking glass" emerge frequently following H.D.'s Pre-Raphaelite revival." Elizabeth Gitter's description of the Pre-Raphaelite origin of this powerful Victorian trope for female, art, sexuality, and narrative, for which Lady Lilith forms a type, might apply to H.D.'s Mary Magdalene:

Silent, the larger-than-life woman who dominated the literature and art of the [Victorian] period used her hair to weave her dis-course . . . at times to shelter her lovers [and] at times to strangle them. But always, as Rossetti's *Lady Lilith* painting suggests, the grand woman achieved her transcendent vitality partly through her magic hair, which was invested with independent energy: enchanting—and enchanted—her gleaming tresses both expressed her mythic power and were its source.

> —Cassandra Laity, "Feminine Abjection and *Trilogy.*" *H.D. and the Victorian Fin De Siècle,* (New York: Cambridge University Press, 1996): pp. 179–181.

JOSEPH RIDDEL ON ORIGIN IN H.D.'S WORK

[Joseph Riddel is the author of several books on modernism. In this essay, he examines the origin of images and H.D.'s metaphor of the hieroglyph, ideas she uncovered while working with Freud.]

The understanding of H.D.'s poetics—and in a sense the thrust of poetic modernism—must be situated in this problematic of the oracular sign and in the question of style (or styles), of the hieroglyph, of dream-writing. Like the metaphysical readings of Heraclitus, which give us a decidable either/or reading yet acknowledge that the oracle's wisdom exceeds the limits of human understanding, H.D.'s poetics has been interpreted in terms of prophecy or mystical revelations, as an archeological uncovering of the secrets concealed in ancient words or texts. Norman Pearson writes in his introduction to the posthumously published *Hermetic Definition*, "Like many Freudians, she became quasi-Jungian and could bring the cabala, astrology, magic, Christianity, classical and Egyptian mythology, and personal experience into a joint sense of Ancient Wisdom" (vi). The cabala, however, and we have only to witness Harold Bloom's appropriation of it, is not necessarily a mystical text of revelations or even a dream book, but only a machine for interpretation, and hence for misprision. H.D.'s alleged Jungianism, and mysticism, is the issue of a blind or idealized reading of her texts that ignores her own problematizing of the image, her own deployment of the text as an analytic. The play between deconstruction and reconstruction, in both her poems and her prose, characterizes (literally and figuratively) this problematic. If for her a poem affirms by *feeling* "the meaning that words hide," that words are "anagrams, cryptograms, / little boxes, conditioned // to hatch butterflies," their revelation is never direct or simple; the poem always remains "jottings on a margin, / indecipherable palimpsest scribbled over // with too many contradictory emotions" (*Trilogy*, 53, 42). The image is never congruent with its origin, its origin never evident outside of the images doubling or distorting, and hence dispersing it. The unconscious is not a reservoir of some untapped truth, but a chaos:

> Depth of the sub-conscious spews forth
> too many incongruent monsters
>
> and fixed indigestible matter
> such as shell, pearl; imagery
>
> done to death; perilous ascent,
> ridiculous descent; rhyme, jingle,
>
> overworked assonance, nonsense,
> juxtaposition of words for words' sake,
>
> without meaning, undefined . . .
> (*Trilogy,* 44)

The poem originates in a place (or a scene) of extraordinary heterogeneity, and proceeds not by opening or unconcealing, but by layering. Yet, it can never reconstruct an original model, let alone a simple origin, or recuperate some original whole, since any notion of the origin (as represented, say, in the "family-complex" by the home) is already only one of the images. Reconstruction involves reading/writing, translation, and distortion. Every poem reveals its own operation, or describes its own sense, therefore, because it conceals by revealing, reveals by concealing. A passage in *The Flowering of the Rod* says it with concise ambivalence:

> And no one will ever know
> whether the picture he saw clearly
>
> as in a mirror was pre-determined
> by his discipline and study
>
> of old lore and by his innate capacity
> for transcribing and translating
>
> the difficult secret symbols

> . . . .
> no one will ever know
> whether it was a sort of spiritual optical illusion,
> or whether he looked down the deep deep-well
>
> of the so-far unknown
> depths of pre-history . . .
> (*Trilogy*, 165)

She is probably allegorizing Freud and/or Pound here, as the Magus to whom she is a Mary, but the allusion is of little matter. In the *Tribute*, the central dreams—the princess dreams and the "Writing on the Wall"—signify the same question, since they have no bottom, no origin in a single event, but originate in what is already a hieroglyph or maimed text. They begin, as at Delphi or at the writing desk, in a double reading/writing of the sign:

> *Signet*—as from sign, a mark, token, proof; signet—the privy seal, a seal; signet-ring—a ring with a signet or private seal; sign-manuel—the royal signature, usually a mention of the sovereign's name. (I have used my initials H.D. consistently as my writing signet or sign-manuel, though it is only, at this moment, as I checked up on the word 'signet' in my Chambers' English Dictionary that I realized that my writing signature has anything remotely suggesting sovereignty or the royal manner.) Sign again—a word, gesture, symbol, or mark, intended to signify something else. Sign again—(medical) a symptom, (astronomical) one of the twelve parts of the Zodiac. (*Tribute*, 66)

H.D.'s "writing on the wall" dream is never interpreted, except as a question of the sign, which must always be read in "two ways or in more than two ways": either as the "suppressed desire for 'signs and wonders'" and hence as the "suppressed desire to be a Prophetess"; or as mere illustration or representations, images borrowed from an actual dream to "*echo*" an idea (*Tribute*, 51). Yet this last is not simple representation or expression but something like a dreamwork which reworks a repression, thus protecting against a "freak" idea or "dangerous symptom." Poetry need not be identified with neurosis, but it is never immediate, and always a distortion or reworking of other images. Poetry, like Freud's "complex," is

Mosaic. One may desire to read it as containing one symbol that determines all the others, like the "sun" of H.D.'s hieroglyphic "Writing on the Wall," but no sign can be extricated as central or singular. It can only be "read," and this reading always involves another, just as does any scene of analysis (*Tribute*, 56).

—Joseph Riddel, "H.D. and Freud." In *The Turning Word: American Literary Modernism and Continental Theory*, (Philadelphia: University of Pennsylvania Press, 1996): pp. 40–43.

LISA RADO ON H.D. AND MALE AUTHORITY

[Lisa Rado teaches at the Harvard-Westlake School in Los Angeles. She is the author of *Modernism, Gender and Culture* and *Rereading Modernism: New Directions in Feminist Criticism*. Here, she discusses failure to create an androgynous overmind and truly transcend male authority.]

If Julia cannot imagine creative transcendence without some connection to the male, neither can the heroines of H.D.'s most famous sequence poems, *Trilogy* and *Helen in Egypt*. Once again, the feminist critics who have written on the poems conclude, with Donna Krolik Hollenberg, that they thematize "the de-idealization of the father and recovery of the mother's power" (125). Yet despite the appearance of the seeming muse-like Lady in *Trilogy* ("Tribute to the Angels," verse 25), the legacy of Freud means that H.D. shows Mary Magdalene (in *Trilogy*) and Helen (of *Helen in Egypt*) as needing to unite with Kaspar and Theseus/Achilles in order to reach their imaginative potentials. While the poet of *Trilogy* desires to "recover the secret of Isis" (54) in order to experience "union at last" within her consciousness (57), what she ends up with is the "unsatisfied duality" (72) of Kaspar and Mary Magdelene (modeled at least in part on Freud and H.D.). While Kaspar does come to see the falsity of his sexist attitudes, the absurdity of believing that "one jar was better than the other" (168), it is he—not Mary—who is granted the moment of vision at the end of the poem:

he saw what the sacrosanct legend
said still existed,

he saw the lands of the blest,
the promised lands, lost;

he, in that half-second, saw
the whole scope and plan

of our and his civilization on this,
his and our earth, before Adam.

("The Flowering of the Rod," verse 31)

Having, by the end of the poem, seen "deeper, apprehended more
than anyone before or after him" (verse 40), Kaspar serves as a
marked contrast to the "shy and simple and young" Mary Magdelene
(verse 43). Moreover, it cannot be ignored that it is ironically he who
recognizes her potential, not Mary herself. For when she remarks
that Kaspar's gift to the Christ child has "a most beautiful fragrance
as of all flowering things together," she does not realize that the
magical, transcendent scent comes from her own gift:

but Kaspar knew the seal of the jar was unbroken.
he did not know whether she knew

the fragrance came from the bundle of myrrh
she held in her arms.

("The Flowering of the Rod," verse 43)

—Lisa Rado, "'The Perfection of the Fiery Moment': H.D.and the
Androgynous Poetics of Overmind." *The Modern Androgyne
Imagination: A Failed Sublime*, (Charlottesville: University Press of
Virginia, 2000): pp. 96–97.

Works by
H.D.

Sea Garden, 1916.

The Tribute and Circe: Two Poems, 1917.

Hymen, 1921.

Heliodora & Other Poems, 1924.

Collected Poems of H.D., 1925.

H.D., 1926.

Palimpsest, 1926.

Hippolytus Temporizes, 1927.

Hedylus, 1928.

Borderline—A Pool Film with Paul Robeson, 1930.

Red Roses for Bronze, 1931.

Kora and Ka, 1934.

The Usual Star, 1934.

Nights, as John Helforth, 1935.

The Hedgehog, 1936.

The Walls Do Not Fall, 1944.

What Do I Love?, 1944.

Tribute to the Angels, 1945.

The Flowering of the Rod, 1946.

By Avon River, 1949.

Tribute to Freud, 1956.

Selected Poems of H.D., 1957.

Bid Me To Live (A Madrigal), 1960.

Helen in Egypt, 1961.

Hermetic Definition, unauthorized 1971, authorized 1972.

Temple of the Sun, 1972.

Trilogy: The Walls Do Not Fall, Tribute to Angels, The Flowering of the Rod, 1973.

The Poet & The Dancer, 1975.

End to Torment: A Memoir of Ezra Pound, 1979.

HERmione, 1981.

The Gift, 1982.

Notes on Thoughts and Vision & the Wise Sappho, 1982.

Collected Poems, 1912–1944, edited by Louis L. Martz, 1983.

Priest and A Dead Priestess Speaks, 1983.

Selected Poems, edited by Louis L. Martz, 1988.

Paint It Today, edited by Cassandra Laity, 1992.

Choruses from Iphigenia in Aulis and Hippolytus of Euripides, translated by Doolittle, 1919.

Euripides' Ion, translated by H.D., 1937.

Vale Ave in *New Directions in Poetry and Prose,* no. 44, 1982.

Works about

H . D .

Ahearn, Barry. "Williams and H.D., or Sour Grapes." *Twentieth Century Literature* 35 (Fall 1989): pp. 299–309.

Arthur, Marilyn. "Psycho-Mythology: The Case of H.D." *Bucknell Review* 28 (1983): pp. 65–79.

Bloom, Harold, ed. *Modern Critical Views: H.D.* New York: Chelsea House, 1989.

Buck, Claire. *H.D. & Freud: Bisexuality and a Feminine Discourse.* New York: Harvester Wheatsheaf, 1991.

Burnett, Gary. *H.D. between Image and Epic The Mysteries of Her Poetics.* Ann Arbor: University of Michigan Research Press, 1990.

Chisholm, Dianne. *H.D.'s Freudian Poetics: Psychoanalysis in Translation.* Ithaca, NY: Cornell University Press, 1992.

Collecott, Diana. *H.D. and Sapphic Modernism.* New York: Cambridge University Press, 1999.

Copeland, Donna. "Doolittle's 'Helen.'" *The Explicator* 46:4 (Summer 1998): pp. 33–35.

Cutler, Carolyn. "Words and Images in H.D.'s *Tribute to Freud.*" *Psychoanalytic Review* 76 (Spring 1989): pp. 107–113.

DiPace Fritz, Angela. *Thought and Vision: A Critical Reading of H.D.'s Poetry.* Washington, D.C.: Catholic University Press, 1988.

Doyle, Charles. "Palimpsests of the Word: The Poetry of H.D. *Queen's Quarterly* 92/93 (Summer 1995): pp. 310–321.

Duncan, Robert. "Beginnings: Chapter 1 of the H.D. Book, Part 1." *Coyote's Journal 5/6* (1967): pp. 6–34.

———. "The H.D. Book, Part 1: Chapter 2." *Coyote's Journal* 8 (1967): pp. 27–35.

———. "Rites of Participation." *Caterpillar* 1 (October 1967): pp. 6–34.

———. "Rites of Participation, II." *Caterpillar* 2 (January 1968): pp. 125–54.

———. "Two Chapters from *H.D.*" *Triquarterly* 12 (Spring 1968): pp. 67–98.

———. "H.D.'s Challenge." *Poesis* 6 (1985): pp. 21–35.

DuPlessis, Rachel Blau. "Romantic Thralldom in H.D." *Contemporary Literature* 20:2 (1979): pp. 178–203.

———. "Family, Sexes, Psyche: An Essay on H.D. and the Muse of the Woman Writer." *Montemora* 6 (1979): pp. 137–156.

———. *H.D.: The Career of that Struggle*. Brighton: Harvester, 1986.

Edmunds, Susan. *Out of Line: History, Psychoanalysis & Montage in H.D.'s Long Poems*. Stanford, CA: Stanford University Press, 1994.

Engel, Bernard F. "H.D.: Poems That Matter and Dilutations." *Contemporary Literature* 10:4 (Autumn 1969): pp. 507–522.

Friebert, L.M. "Conflict and Creativity in the World of H.D." *Journal of Women's Studies in Literature I*, no. 3 (Summer 1979): pp. 258–271.

Friedman, Susan Stanford. "Who Buried H.D.? A Poet, Her Critics and Her Place in the Literary Tradition." *College English* 36, no. 7 (1975): pp.801–814.

———. *Psyche Reborn: The Emergence of H.D.* Bloomington: Indiana University Press, 1981.

———. *Penelope's Web*: *Gender, Modernity, H.D.'s Fiction*. New York: Cambridge University Press, 1990.

Friedman, Susan Stanford and Rachel Blau DuPlessis, eds. *Signets: Reading H.D.* Madison: University of Wisconsin Press, 1990.

Gelpi, Albert. "Re-membering the Mother: A Reading of H.D.'s *Trilogy*." *Poesis* 6 (1985): pp. 40–57.

Gibbons, Kathryn Gibbs. "The Art of H.D." *The Mississippi Quarterly* 15:4 (Fall 1962): pp. 152–160.

Gregory, Eileen. "Scarlet Experience: H.D.'s *Hymen*." *Sagetrieb* 6:2 (Fall 1987): pp. 77–100.

————. *H.D. and Hellenism*. New York: Cambridge University Press, 1997.

Gubar, Susan. "The Echoing Spell of H.D.'s *Trilogy*." *Contemporary Literature* 19:2 (Spring 1978): pp.196–218.

————. "Sapphistries." *Signs* 10 (Autumn 1984): pp. 43–62.

Guest, Barbara. *Herself Defined: The Poet H.D. and Her World*. Garden City, NY: Doubleday, 1984.

Holland, Norman. *Poems in Persons*. New York: Norton, 1973.

Hollenberg, Donna Krolik, ed. *Between History and Poetry: The Letters of H.D. and Norman Holmes Pearson*. Iowa City: University of Iowa Press, 1997.

————. *H.D.: The Poetics of Childbirth and Creativity*. Boston: Northeastern University Press, 1991.

Kelvin, Norman. "H.D. and the Years of World War I." *Victorican Poetry* 38:1 (2000) 170–196.

King, Michael, ed. *H.D.: Woman and Poet*. Orono, ME: National Poetry Foundation, 1986.

Kloepfer, Deborah Kelly. *The Unspeakable Mother: Forbidden Discourse in Jean Rhys and H.D.* Ithaca: Cornell University Press, 1989.

Laity, Cassandra. "H.D.'s Romantic Landscapes: The Sexual Politics of the Garden." *Sagetrieb* 6:2 (Fall 1987): pp. 57–76.

————. *H.D. and the Victorian Fin De Siecle*. NY: Cambridge University Press, 1996.

Levertov, Denise. "H.D.: An Appreciation." *Poetry* 100 (June 1962) 182–186.

Lowell, Amy. *Tendencies in Modern American Poetry*. NY: Macmillan, 1917: pp. 235–243.

Martz, Louis L. "H.D.: Set Free to Prophesy." *Many Gods and Many Voices: The Role of the Prophet in English and American Modernism*. Columbia: University of Missouri, 1998: pp. 80–108.

————. "H.D. and D.H." *Many Gods and Many Voices: The Role of the Prophet in English and American Modernism*. Columbia: University of Missouri Press, 1998: 109–129.

Mathis, Mary S. *H.D.: An Annotated Bibliography, 1913–1986.* Boston: Garland, 1991.

Morris, Adalaide. "The Concept of Projection: H.D.'s Visionary Powers." *Contemporary Literature* 25 (Winter 1984): pp. 411–36.

Ostriker, Alicia. "No Rules of Procedure: The Open Poetics of H.D." *Agenda* 25 (Autumn/Winter 1987–88): pp. 145–154.

Pondrum, Cyrena. "H.D. and the Origins of Imagism." *Sagetrieb* 4, no. 1 (Spring 1985): pp.73–100.

Pratt, William, ed. *The Imagist Poem.* New York: Dutton, 1963.

Quinn, Vincent. "H.D.'s 'Hermetic Definition:' The Poet as Archetypal Mother." *Contemporary Literature* 18:1 (1977): pp. 51–61.

———. *Hilda Doolittle.* NY: Twayne, 1967.

Rado, Lisa. *The Modern Androgyne Imagination*: *A Failed Sublime.* Charlottesville: University Press of Virginia, 2000: pp. 60–98.

Rainey, Lawrence. "Patronage and the Poetics of the Coterie: H.D. in the Modernist Canon." *Institutions of Modernism: Literary Elites and Public Culture.* New Haven: Yale University Press, 1998.

Rich, Adrienne. "When We Dead Awaken: Writing as Re-Vision." *On Lies, Secrets, and Silences: Prose.* NY: Norton, 1979: pp. 33–49.

Riddel, Joseph. "H.D. and Freud." *The Turning Word: American Literary Modernism and Continental Theory.* Philadelphia: University of Pennsylvania Press, 1996.

Robinson, Janice S. *H.D.: The Life and Work of an American Poet.* Boston: Houghton Mifflin, 1982.

Showalter, Elaine. "Feminist Criticism in the Wilderness." *New Feminist Criticism.* ed. Elaine Showalter. New York: Pantheon, 1985: pp. 243–270.

Sword, Helen. *Engendering Inspiration.* Ann Arbor: University of Michigan Press, 1995.

Swann, Thomas Burnett. *The Classical World of H.D.* Lincoln: University of Nebraska Press, 1962.

Taylor, Georgina. *H.D. and the Public Sphere of Modernist Women Writers, 1913–1946: Talking Women*. NY: Oxford University Press, 2001.

Triglio, Tony. *"Strange Prophecies Anew": Rereading Apocalypse in Blake, H.D. and Ginsberg*. Madison, N.J.: Farleigh Dickinson University Press, 2001.

Watts, H.H. "H.D. and the Age of Myth." *The Sewanee Review* 56 (Spring 1948): pp. 287–303.

ACKNOWLEDGMENTS

"'Priapus' and 'Hermes'" by Janice S. Robinson © 1982 from *H.D.: The Life and Work of an American Poet* by Houghton Mifflin. Reprinted by Permission.

"H.D. and the Origins of Imagism" by Cyrena N. Pondrom © 1985 from *Sagtrieb* 4:1. Reprinted by Permission.

"H.D.'s Romantic Landscapes: The Sexual Politics of the Garden" by Cassandra Laity © 1987 from *Sagetrieb* 6:2. Reprinted by Permission.

"H.D. and the Classical Lyric" by Eileen Gregory © 1997 from *H.D. and Hellenism: Classical Lines* by Cambridge University Press. Reprinted by Permission.

"Sapphistries" by Susan Gubar © 1984 from *Signs* 10:1 by The University of Chicago Press. Reprinted by Permission.

"H.D.'s Imagism: A Poetry of Loss and Rebellion" from *H.D.: The Poetics of Childbirth and Creativity* by Donna Krolik Hollenberg. Copyright 1991 by Donna Krolik Hollenberg. Reprinted with the Permission of Northeastern University Press.

"H.D. and the Poetics of Possession" by Helen Sword © 1995 from *Engendering Inspiration: Visionary Strategies in Rilke, Lawrence, and H.D.* by University of Michigan Press. Reprinted by Permission.

"'the art of the future:' Her Emergence from Imagism" by Diana Collecott © 1999 from *H.D. and Sapphic Modernism, 1910-1950* by Cambridge University Press. Reprinted by Permission.

"Born of One Mother: Re-Vision of Patriarchal Tradition" by Susan Stanford Friedman © 1981 from *Psyche Reborn: The Emergence of H.D.* by Indiana University Press. Reprinted by Permission.

The Explicator, 46:4, 1988. Reprinted with permission of the Helen Dwight Reid Education Froundation. Published by Heldref Publications, 1319 Eighteenth St., NW Washington, DC 20036-1802 © 1988.

Themes and Ideas

"GIFT, THE", 28

H.D.: biography of, 14-17; claim to superstition, 42-46; development of modern lyric, 36-37; on Greek Anthology, 28-30; iconic role of Sappho in writing, 42-46; love in poetry, 39-40; as mythmaker, 68; as a precursor, 75-77; her poetics, 90-93, 116-119; relationship with Pound, 22-23, 26; 'white' state in poetry, 37-39;

"HELEN", 49-61; absolution of emotion, 50-51; aftermath of war, 50; autobiographical subject in, 61; celebration of lesbian love in, 58-59; contrasts in, 57; critical analysis of, 49-52; critical views of, 53-61; dead beauty vs. live beauty in, 51-52; Greek Myth in, 49-61; and *Helen in Egypt*, 52, 59-60; Helen of Troy, 49-61, and canonization of, 56, and as heroic, 59-61, and imagery of, 53-55; inner voice in, 52, 59-60; and Medusa, 56; patriarchal cage in, 56, 58-59; and Poe's Helen, 54; relationship to tradition, 55; as symbol of Greece, 56-58; symbolism of sexual beauty and illicit love, 53-54, 57-58; textual metaphors, 60; transformation in, 53; victim in, 52, 'white' in, 50, 55; word meaning in, 54-55

HELIODORA, 39, 46

"HERMES OF THE WAYS", 29

"HERMONAX", 29

HYMEN, 31, 37-39

"LEDA", 39

"ORCHARD", 18-30; and Aldington's "Choricos", 23-24; Christian myth in, 21; conflicting emotions in, 25; critical analysis of, 18-21; critical views of, 22-30; direct object of, 21; emotion of God's appeal, 20-21; the fall in, 21, 24-25; fallen fruit in, 20-21, 24-26; Greek Myth in, 18-19, 22-24, 28, 30; as hallmark, 26; humor and irony in, 22-23; imagery in, 18, 26-27; love in, 24; lover paradise in, 28; offering in, 25-26; and Paton's *Anthology*, 22; Priapus in, 19-23; psychic paralysis in, 27-28; quest of the bees, 19-20; setting, 19; sexual subtext in, 26; stormy landscape, 27-28; subtitle of, 18, 24; treatment of the 'thing', 18; troubadour tradition in, 22-23

SEA GARDEN, 27-28

"SHELTERED GARDEN", 27